newcanvaswork

newcanvaswork
creative techniques in needlepoint

JILL CARTER

BATSFORD

For Isadora and Milo

Acknowledgements

Special thanks go to my skilled colleagues, friends and students who have so generously lent me their embroideries and permitted them to be included in this book, and especially Pam Watts for her support and encouragement.

Thank you to Tina Persaud and her team at Batsford, in particular my editor Karen Dolan, for making the book happen, and to Michael Wicks for his superb photography.

Finally, thanks to DMC for generously supplying some of the materials used in the book.

First published in Great Britain in 2007 by
Batsford
151 Freston Road
London W10 6TH

An imprint of Anova Books Company Ltd

ISBN-13: 9780713489750

A CIP catalogue record for this book is available from the British Library.

10 9 8 7 6 5 4 3 2 1

Reproduction by Anorax Imaging Limited, Leeds
Printed and bound by Craft Print International Limited, Singapore

This book can be ordered direct from the publisher at the website:
www.anovabooks.com, or try your local bookshop

Photography by Michael Wicks

Previous pages
Red Cushions (Jill Carter) with free straight stitch machining over the corners of reversed cushion stitch formed into squares. The squares are divided by a laid novelty yarn, combined with double knot stitch for extra texture, and then overstitched with a free machined decorative pattern.

Contents

Introduction   6

1   Materials   8

2   Background surfaces (or treatments)   18

3   Colour, design and stitch   30

4   Couching on a canvas background   46

5   Embroidery stitches on canvas   52

6   Applying objects onto a canvas background   60

7   Drawn-thread techniques on canvas   70

8   Pulled thread on canvas   76

9   Machine embroidery on canvas   82

10 Beads and stitches on canvas   96

11 Background stitching for canvas work   106

12 Finishing techniques   116

Stitches   124

Equipment and materials & Further reading   126

Index   128

Introduction

Today's canvas work (also known as needlepoint) can be anything you want it to be, so banish any of your preconceived ideas of it being restrictive and take pleasure in all that is canvas. Using a fresh and contemporary approach to canvas work becomes a powerful means of self-expression and will offer you compelling and irresistible challenges.

The sheer volume and inexhaustible variety of imaginative stitches will keep you inspired and sewing for a lifetime, whether it is for free interpretation or to make the most of pattern. Add to this the astounding selection of breathtaking threads of any texture you could possibly think of, or want – and you will definitely be hooked. The diversity of threads has done much to act as a catalyst to stimulate creativity, innovation and considerable artistry, and altogether revolutionize the way we approach canvas work.

My book is a celebration of canvas work and all that you can take advantage of and accomplish on an even-weave background canvas – from the traditional to the contemporary. Within the arena of contemporary canvas work there are few restraints and I trust that with a little help from the book, whether you are a novice or an expert, you will want to consider new challenges and augment your skills to experiment with paint and colour, explore line and shape and research a range of textures. I will take you on a journey with a comprehensive overview of integrating canvas work and other embroidery techniques that will translate well with canvas, with chapters on couching and laid fillings, basic embroidery stitches, drawn and pulled thread techniques, appliqué, backgrounds and finishing techniques – and more. Perhaps you are a beader who may chance upon a whole new path for exhibiting your beading skills, or maybe you are a machine embroiderer who will discover new possibilities for broadening your expertise as you combine machining with hand stitching on canvas.

Whatever your passion in stitching, I hope that this book will inspire you to dabble in the abstract, adventure into the contemporary or simply enjoy the pleasure of filling spaces and interpreting the representational, to discover a potpourri of glorious colour, texture and stitch on canvas.

Applying objects with needleweaving techniques. On a background textured with wools, threads and strips of fabric were woven through the canvas and used to make double knot stitch and French knots. Areas were overstitched with free machining granite stitch and random fly stitch. Long-armed cross stitch reveals the background canvas as a contrast to the solid central area, with beads for an added dimension.

1 Materials

CANVAS

Canvas work embroidery is traditionally stitched on an even-weave grid of cotton fibres, which are stiffened with a specially formulated 'sizing' to form what is familiarly known to embroiderers as canvas. There are three main types – double, mono and interlock. Other fabrics of an even-weave nature may also be used with canvas work stitches, from moulded grids of plastic or vinyl, Congress cloth or even-weave linens to the finest of silk gauze. Although canvas is considered an even-weave fabric, a slight variance will show in measurement – the warp is the accurate measurement with the weft being marginally larger.

The quality of canvas varies, and it is always worth buying the best that you can afford as this will be the basis for your embroidery into which you will be putting a lot of time and effort. A 'polished' canvas will be easier to sew. Polishing buffs away the small hairs of the background to produce a smooth canvas, which means that sewing threads do not get 'plucked' as the stitches are made. Canvas comes in a variety of colours depending on the type and count of the canvas. It is mostly found in white and antique, but there is a range of colours in Congress cloth, interlock canvas and in 18-count mono canvas including black in 18- and 12-count mono.

A **Penelope or double-mesh canvas** is woven vertically and horizontally with pairs of threads. The canvas may be trammed for wearability and coverage, but with the size of mesh come some limitations as to the choice of stitch. Long stitches on a larger count of canvas may snag and be inappropriate for your project. Tent stitch can be used for emphasis or detailing over a single thread.

Double-mesh canvas

Single canvas

A **mono or single canvas** is woven vertically and horizontally with a single thread and will give you scope for using almost any canvas work stitch you wish and will suit most projects.

An **interlock canvas** has the warp thread wrapping and 'locking' the weft thread to make the fabric stable. This canvas is often a cheaper option than other types of canvas, but it is worth remembering that it is generally not as strong and durable as a single or double mesh canvas. However, it is useful for three-dimensional work, as folded edges are not so bulky and areas of the canvas may be cut out without completely unravelling.

Plastic/vinyl canvas consists of a moulded grid and lends itself to structured pieces and a variety of three-dimensional projects. It comes in rectangular sheets and other geometric shapes and will not fray when cut away. Vinyl grids have double or single mesh.

Congress cloth is a finer, stiffened even-weave cotton that works well for detailed canvas work embroidery. It can be found in a variety of colours but test for colour-fastness before using.

Silk gauze is used for miniatures or applied pieces and comes in white, natural and black.

A selection of canvases including plastic, rug, double, mono, interlocking and Congress cloth.

Waste canvas is generally double mesh. It is placed on a background fabric and overstitched with canvas work stitches on the even-weave construction. The threads are then dampened and withdrawn, leaving the canvas work stitches in place on the background fabric.

Canvas count

The size of the canvas mesh is the significant factor in canvas work and determines the final size of the stitches. The count is the number of threads to the inch (2.5 cm), which go to make up the mesh. It is important to buy the size most appropriate to the type of project being embarked upon, one that is relevant to the type of threads being used and of a size of mesh that you can see. The fewer the number of threads to the inch/2.5 cm the larger the even-weave grid and, therefore, the resulting stitches. Canvas can be found in counts from 3 threads to the inch (rug) to 22, Congress cloth from 22 to 24 and silk gauze upwards from 18 to 40.

TIPS

- Stitch with the grain of the canvas for smoother and more uniform stitches.
- To find the grain of the canvas, the selvage should be on the west or east side of your stitching, so that the weft threads travel west-east and the warp threads travel north-south.
- Without a selvage, find the grain of the canvas by pulling out a vertical and horizontal thread. The more wrinkled thread is the warp.

CREATIVE IDEAS

If you would like to try out a new concept and use different gridded background fabrics, not only can you create your own grids with your choice of fibres, but you will be amazed at how many unusual types you will be able to find. As well as being possible background grids, some may also be applied onto canvas or incorporated as an integral part of your design. Experiment and look around for some of the following:

A variety of gridded textures including paper, fabric, acrylic and plant fibres.

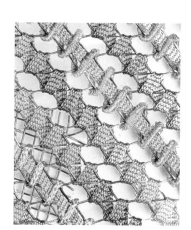

- **Wire mesh** – This can be discovered (generally rust proof) in lengths or manageable sheets with grids of different sizes in copper, brass, aluminium and stainless steel. It is quite flexible and can be cut with scissors, stitched, manipulated, folded, pleated and coloured. Covering the raw edges with tape will protect your thread and fingers while you are stitching. A fine thread used for canvas stitches on the mesh will allow the background patina of the metal to reflect through. Using a thicker thread to block the sheen will help to contrast and emphasize the areas of lustre.
- **Paper** – Grids of different dimensions can be found in paper products, and are perfectly easy to stitch on. Work some small practice stitch samples before embarking on a finished piece to check that the stitches work. Stitch holes made in paper are difficult to disguise if you have a change of heart. Paper can easily be applied and incorporated onto canvas. Ribbons of wired paper mesh also work well for surface application or manipulating.
- **Raffia and other plant fibres** – Interestingly coloured and textured grids of different thicknesses can be sourced made with raffia and other such plant fibres. These products are quite floppy, but can be stitched using a frame to keep them taut.

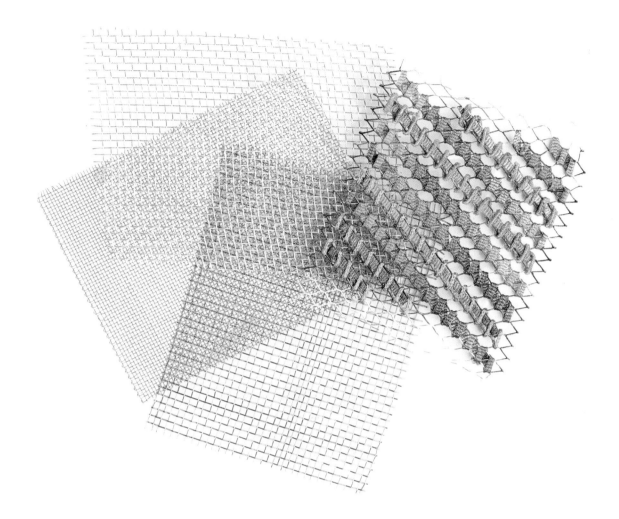

A variety of wire mesh sheets useful for hand stitching, which can then be applied or manipulated into any required shape or area.

- **Knitting** – Using different gauge needles and weight of wool/fibres will offer an enormous range of textures and size of mesh to develop for stitching, machining or manipulating onto canvas. Choose a simple unpatterned stitch such as plain or purl to knit, and practise on a sample piece first.
- **Crochet** – Grids of crochet can be created with single or double chains, and varying the size of hook and thread will give you a change in mesh size. Crocheting with yarn combined with a fine wire will give the piece some rigidity for stitching or later manipulating a texture onto canvas.
- **Creating your own grid with specially chosen yarns** – Choosing your own yarns to make a background grid offers all manner of opportunities for creating the exact colour, texture and size to suit your needs for an experimental piece. Yarns for the surface stitching would have to be of a size and texture to show up on the background and give the maximum impact. If necessary a solution of PVA glue could be painted onto the back of your grid to stiffen it, and it could be incorporated with a normal canvas background for a dramatic contemporary wall hanging. Create such a grid as follows:

1. Position drawing pins (thumb tacks) the chosen distance apart on a wooden frame. You will be fixing the warp and weft threads to these, attaching each one with a knot.
2. Attach the warp threads to the frame first and then weave the weft threads in and out of the warp.

THREADS

Traditionally wool is used in canvas work – either tapestry, crewel or Persian - and consideration should always be given to using the correct weight of wool for canvas and stitch if you are working on a traditional piece. Even if you are working in a traditional manner, it does not preclude you from embracing some of the contemporary threads now available to us, unless the project is for upholstery, when it is preferable to use the correct wools for durability.

The perception of canvas work has changed. If a yarn, thread or other item will go through the canvas or is suitable for couching, try it. Adapt your canvas gauge if necessary to suit the thread. Embroiderers are striving to experiment and include all sorts of different effects and textures in their work to make the most of what is available.

The texture and colour of today's threads will inspire you to stitch. The choice is intoxicating with a thrilling profusion of different types of thread and infinite colours. There are the usual cottons (stranded, perles, etc.), silks, rayons, ribbons, metallics, machine threads and knitting yarns, and even within this wonderful array of threads, the colours and combinations have

Various standard and novelty yarns can be included on canvas and mixed with the more usually accepted fibres.

multiplied – plain and shaded threads abound. Tantalizing hand-dyed plain and shaded wools, angoras, mohairs, silks, cottons, linens, synthetics and ribbons can be found in different thicknesses and scrumptious textures. Combinations of fibres, such as wool and silk, silk and cotton or wool and rayon, add to the range. The selection and colour variation of metallic threads, twists, cords, ribbons and braids is vast and breathtaking. Moving into the more contemporary styles, you will find knitting, textured and novelty yarns, unusual machine embroidery threads and plant fibres such as banana, jute, hemp or linen, which could also be used and incorporated into canvas work. Texture and colour make the buying of threads irresistible to the canvas work enthusiast.

TIPS

• If you use space-dyed/shaded threads, work a sample to ensure that the colours do not 'bleed' when the work is dampened for stretching. Stitch your colours next to white stitches, wet the sample and check the colours do not run into the white.

• Cut the new length of thread to follow on from the last cutting so that the colours continue to flow in sequence, unless you want otherwise.

• When you are using hanks of wool, such as Appletons, cut into three equal lengths. The threads are too long if the hank is cut in half and too short if cut in quarters. Make the first cut in the circle of wool and then divide the open length equally into three, and cut top and bottom. Always take new lengths of wool from the same end each time.

• Check the twist of the wool and sew with the twist and not against it.

Selection of metallic threads, silk and wire suitable for hand stitching on canvas.

NEEDLES

Tapestry needles are used for canvas work, as they have blunt points and long eyes. The size of the needle you need is governed by the size of the canvas mesh and thread being used. It should be possible to pull the needle through the hole without a struggle. Equally the needle should not drop through the canvas holes. In addition the thread should pass through the eye easily without falling out. Certain threads, such as metallic ones, are tricky to keep in the needle, but instructions for secure threading are usually given on the packet by the manufacturer. It is also sometimes helpful to use a chenille needle when stitching ribbons or difficult novelty yarns. The point of the needle can be brought back through the newly threaded yarn, just a short distance from the end. Adjust and pull up the yarn so that it is secure in the eye of the needle and will not come unthreaded as you stitch. A larger eyed needle will be convenient for protecting the thread as the needle goes through the hole in the canvas and will allow any strands to splay out and lie flat.

EQUIPMENT

Frames

It is always preferable to use a frame for canvas work no matter what claims are made for the different types of canvas. With the techniques that are suggested in this book you will usually find a frame invaluable. Framing will considerably help prevent your work from distorting and, once you are in the rhythm of stabbing the needle from the top to bottom and back again, your tension will become more uniform and the result more professional.

Frame preference is very personal. Frames come in all shapes, sizes and variations to suit most eventualities, but you will probably find that you need a variety. Choice of frames is mostly determined by the size and type of project in hand. A number of plastic frames are available on the market that claim to be suitable for use with canvas, but it has to be remembered that, while these types of frame work admirably for embroidery fabrics, the sizing in some canvases makes them very stiff and therefore difficult to press into place between rings or clips without distortion. On the whole the traditional frames still work the best.

Wooden scroll, roller frames or embroidery 'slate' frames and similar require the canvas to be secured in place with stitching on the two taped sides and tightened with lacing over the two side bars. A refinement of the roller-type frame has a gully into which the canvas and a wooden rod is slotted, necessitating lacing only on the two side bars and needing no other securing stitches. A roller frame will often need to be adjusted and tightened up after stitching. A 'slate' frame, which has not only been slotted tightly into position in one direction, but also laced in the other, usually stays drum-tight and is the most satisfactory surface on which to stitch for good technique and perfect tension.

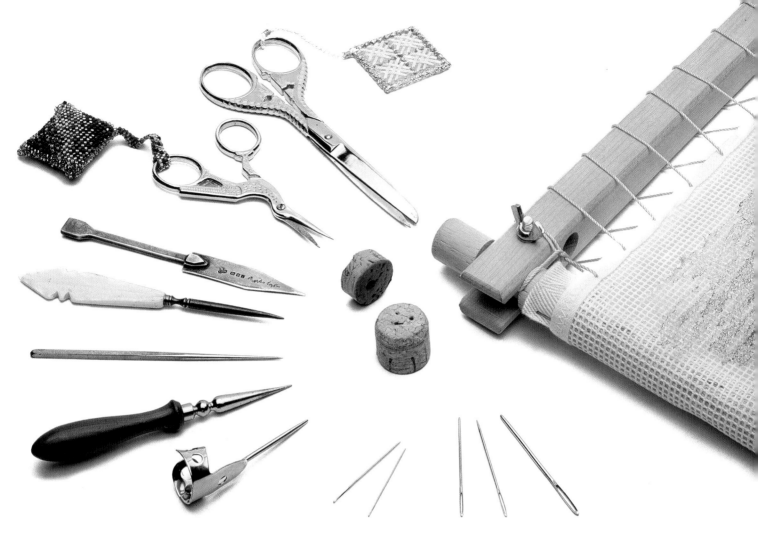

Equipment: a canvas mounted on a roller frame, scissors, mellore (for manipulating metal thread), stilettos (for making holes), laying tools and a selection of needles and pieces of cork to protect any sharp points.

TIPS

- Cover the raw edges of your canvas with fine cotton tape or similar, but preferably not masking tape. Masking tape deteriorates and may leave sticky deposits on the canvas.

- As you wind up unused canvas on a roller frame, insert a small hand towel the width of the canvas, to take up any slack and keep the canvas taut.

Stretcher bars formed into a square or rectangle make quick work of mounting a canvas. They work well for canvas work that cannot be rolled for fear of squashing the thread textures or stitches, and for smaller pieces. The canvas can be stretched and positioned with drawing pins (thumb tacks) or staples. You can vary and customize the size and shape of your frame to suit your requirements exactly by combining different length side bars.

TIPS

- Ensure that the canvas is put on straight with the threads parallel to the bars.
- The canvas will stretch and move with use so readjust the canvas when necessary.
- Ensure the frame is big enough for the piece of canvas to have a border of spare canvas round the design of at least 1½ inches (4 cm).
- Cut the canvas to run along the outer edges of the stretcher bars.

Traditional hand-made, fabric-covered frames with wide, tightly padded sides, where the canvas is secured with heavy-duty pins stabbed though the canvas into the padding, are still being made but are not readily available. They are quite heavy, so more appropriate for smaller projects, especially if you like to work with a stand.

Stands

A stand to hold the frame is a valuable optional extra. It helps with posture and means you have two hands free with which to sew. Made of wood, plastic or metal, some stands sit on the floor, or on your lap, others prop up on the table – again the type and choice is very personal and dependent on the size of the project being undertaken.

Scissors

We all have our favourites, but a small pair of embroidery scissors that cut to the point should be saved for threads and not cutting canvas. Larger sized scissors with serrated edges work wonderfully well for cutting canvas and never seem to blunt. An old pair of embroidery scissors will do well for synthetics, metal threads and metallics.

TIPS

- Do not use a quick unpick (seam ripper) for cutting out unwanted stitches – it is the quickest way of cutting your background canvas.
- Tweezers are good for pulling out unwanted threads.
- Masking tape can be dabbed onto unpicked areas to collect up remaining fluff or small threads.

Laying tools

A laying tool is a specific implement used to lay stranded threads (such as wool, silk, floss or ribbon) smoothly onto the fabric as you stitch. The threads are first smoothed and laid over the laying tool, which stays in place until the tension is pulled up to form the stitch. At the last minute the tool is taken away and the strands are placed flat. Laying tools can be made of metal, wood, bone and plastic, and are generally long, pointed and narrow to enable the stitcher to control the thread until it reaches the background fabric. Whether the tempered steel teko-bari (and similar) with a very sharp point or a beautifully finished piece of wood is used is a matter of preference for the stitcher.

An alternative is a laying tool attached to a thimble or a ring and worn on the finger. There are a number of safety issues with this type, as it is easy to forget that it is attached to your finger on the thimble or ring and to injure yourself or someone else as you move your hand.

If you are unable to find a specific laying tool, a large tapestry needle, knitting needle, bodkin or stiletto will do the job. A stiletto is also useful for dragging across the canvas to check lines of stitches, counting threads and enlarging eyelet holes.

TIPS

- If you are going to use a laying tool, it will be necessary to use both hands; therefore, if you are not working on a stand, you will need a weight or clamp to secure the frame to free your hands.

- Choose a laying tool that suits your hand size without causing cramp and that is suitable for the threads with which you are working.

POSTURE

It is always important to find the correct and most comfortable place for your stitching and to have what you need around you. Always try to work in a good sitting position and in a situation with suitable lighting. If you sew for long stretches, get up and move around and try a few simple exercises to get your circulation going and loosen up your neck and shoulders. Use magnification where you need to.

TRANSFERRING THE DESIGN

The generally accepted methods of transferring a design onto canvas are either to use a lightbox or to tape the design to the window in order to trace through onto the canvas. Both these methods entail marking the design with a heavy outline and transferring the design, by tracing it onto the canvas with a guaranteed waterproof pen or, at a pinch, transfer pens (but never with a lead pencil). Although these methods are useful if you are doing a traditional design, on balance I prefer to 'tissue tack' my design with hand stitching. This means that any changes that you might want to make during the working of the design can be accomplished without the problem of trying to get rid of a dark outline transferred by waterproof pen.

'Tissue tacking' is a simple method of tracing the design onto tissue paper (using a permanent marker), placing the tissue onto the canvas ensuring that it is straight and parallel to the threads in the canvas background, and then tacking carefully through paper and canvas and round all the elements of the design. Imprint the blunt end of the needle carefully over the tacking stitches to separate the paper from the stitches. Work in stages round the design, gently pulling the paper away from the tacking stitches. With the design on the canvas in tacking stitches, you then have the option to make any changes you wish as you progress.

2 Background surfaces (or treatments)

Contemporary canvas work needs contemporary treatments, starting with the background canvas. Altering the background canvas with either colour or texture can greatly enhance the look of your work, especially when you want to break from the traditional or want to show the canvas grid as part of your finished embroidery. The altered background often becomes an added source of inspiration. Stitches and threads can be planned to take full advantage of the interestingly coloured grounds with the effects contrasting with or complementing each other. Painted and textured backgrounds have to be considered within the context of the project being worked. For example, certain painted or textured background techniques would not be appropriate for use on utilitarian items such as a chair seat. Professionally hand-painted/commercially printed designs may be purchased but this book deals with the challenge of making your own in a less structured way.

PAINTED BACKGROUNDS

There are a number of ways of colouring the background canvas, but there must always be an awareness that the canvas has been sized and that the point of the canvas is its rigidity. Dowsing it in paint will dilute the sizing, making it floppy, and will possibly distort the canvas – all well and good if that is the effect required, but in general it is preferable to use methods that do not soak the canvas. As finished canvas work is usually dampened and blocked on completion, ensuring that the background paints are stabilized and will not leach into the threads and stitches is another consideration in choosing which method of painting to use.

Planning the colour scheme of paint and thread is crucial to the success of your project, and first it is helpful to consider and rationalize the reasons for painting the background before starting:

- Is it being painted merely to prevent any of the background colour of the canvas showing up through the stitching?
- Do you want the background colour (or colours) to show up through stitches worked in fine or gold threads?
- Are parts of the design going to be left unstitched to reveal creatively painted areas?
- Is the painting technique you have chosen in sympathy with the stitching?
- Will the painted background act as a contrast or complement the colour scheme?

You will need to adopt the method most suited to the effect you want to create for your final piece.

As with all paint or chemicals, meticulously follow the manufacturer's instructions and take the usual safety precautions: wear a mask and gloves if applicable and work in an open and airy space. Do not take any risks.

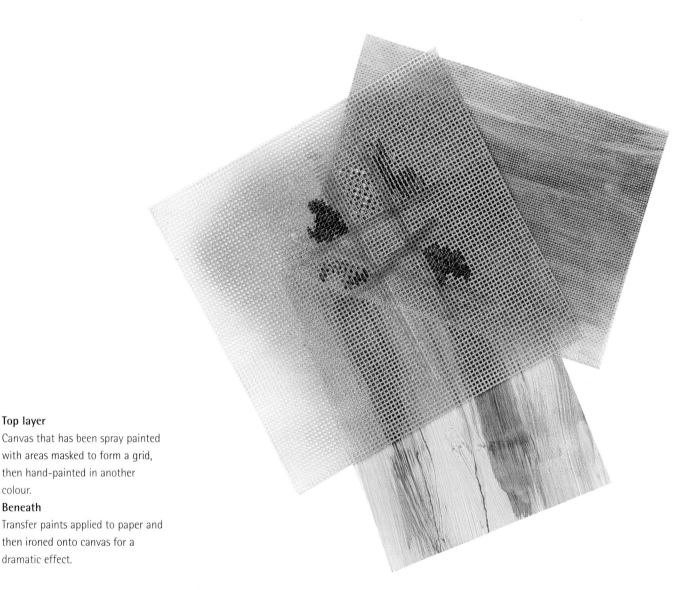

Top layer
Canvas that has been spray painted
with areas masked to form a grid,
then hand-painted in another
colour.

Beneath
Transfer paints applied to paper and
then ironed onto canvas for a
dramatic effect.

Commercial spray paint

Spraying the background with commercial enamel aerosol paint is a useful and quick way of
colouring the canvas, perhaps to tone down the white, or to make the antique canvas look
more interesting. This method works well when you want a speedy all-over effect. Follow the
instructions and spray from a distance in order to achieve even results. Areas can also be
stencilled or masked out according to your design and colour changes. The smell from the paint
can linger on your canvas, and care must be taken by those with allergies. When you are using
metallic sprays, test the colour on a spare piece of canvas, as sometimes the colour is not as
true as it looks on the can lid, especially the golds.

Transfer paints

Transfer paints offer considerable scope for creating appealing or dramatic colour schemes on
the background. Although usually used on fabrics with a synthetic content, transfer paints
transfer well from paper onto canvas. Following the manufacturer's instructions will give you the
basic skills. It is worth painting small colour samples and transferring them onto a piece of
practice canvas to have some notion of the final transferred colour.

The paint is usually applied to a lightweight/non-absorbent paper in whatever pattern you wish. Painting on the paper can be done with a variety of sponges or brushes. Textures can be incorporated, and colours blended. Ironing on the back of your painted paper to transfer the paint onto the canvas will produce differing depths of colour according to how hot the iron is and for how long the piece is ironed – cleverly discreet or overtly bright.

TIP

• When using transfer techniques, remember to protect the ironing board with baking parchment underneath the canvas before you commence ironing.

It is always important to make extra painted papers with which to practise or in case you need more of the same, as you will probably not be able to reproduce the identical effect again. As with other painting methods areas may be blocked out on the canvas with paper shapes, ribbons, flowers or leaves before ironing the transfer-painted papers onto canvas. This would leave outlines free of paint and enable these areas to be left blank or coloured differently. Transfer paintings will also work well on hand-made papers, textured fabrics and webs of fibres and these, in their turn, could be applied or bonded to the background canvas for interesting background effects and textures. The actual resulting colours from transfer painting are not always predictable when used on fabrics/backgrounds for which they were not intended, but, they are often dramatic and may spark other ideas and inspire you to work with unusual colour schemes.

Fabric paints

Fabric paints, including acrylics, silk paints and inks, may be applied directly onto the canvas and work well if you want to sponge or merge colours (remember not to soak the canvas). Fabric paints can also be poured into a pump or trigger spray for spraying or purchased in a pressurised spray can ready to use.

Diluting the paint will give paler effects and gentle colour washes. Using thicker solutions of fabric paint will enable you to block print, stencil or create patterns on the canvas with a brush or sponge or printing block.

Block printing is a very satisfying way of printing randomly on the canvas to give a range of wonderful background impressions of shape or abstract patterns on which to work and can often be the source of inspiration for random stitchery.

Generally the paints just need gentle heat to make them permanent, but always follow the manufacturer's instructions. On the whole I have found that, once paint has been absorbed by the canvas sizing, it is extremely difficult to remove it. As a result you have to ensure the paint goes where you want it.

Markal paint sticks

These oil paint sticks come in a glorious array of colours, including plains, iridescents, glitters and fluorescents. As they are 'dry', the colour is absorbed into the canvas with no requirement for water, which is very useful. The skin forming on the top of the stick has to be peeled or scratched off before it can be used, and then the colour can be rubbed, brushed and worked into the canvas surface or on top of stitches or textures already in place. Interesting effects and shades are achieved when combining and merging different colours.

TIPS

- It is preferable to leave the colouring to dry out for 48 hours before surface stitching.
- Smoother effects are achieved on interlocking canvas, since the canvas lies flatter than the woven single or double-mesh canvas.

Water-soluble pencils/crayons/felt tips

Water-soluble pencils or crayons can be used in most situations but make colouring large areas of canvas rather laborious. They are probably most effective when used to touch up or colour small areas or an area in which, as an afterthought, you need colour. Pulled thread techniques worked on a surface-painted ground may expose small patches of the background canvas that have not absorbed any paint. Colouring the canvas with the pencils or crayons and then spreading the colour with a wet paintbrush or sponge is a quick method of dispersing and merging the colour where it is required. Alternatively, the canvas can be dampened and the colour rubbed into the damp area and then spread as before.

Screen printing

It is possible to screen print your design onto canvas but the process will soften the canvas and it may be necessary to resize it afterwards. This method may be appropriate for a large design on a longer length of canvas and if you have the facilities and equipment for screen printing, but on the whole the other painting methods are more than adequate for colouring the canvas.

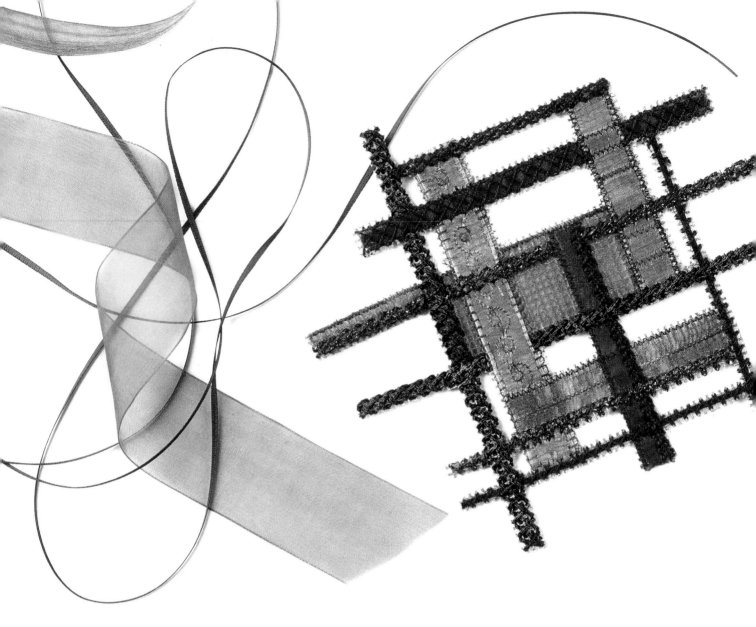

TEXTURES

Painting the background is an obvious starting point, but it becomes even more exciting when combined with different textures. Textures to be applied have to be chosen with care if you still want to use the canvas mesh underneath. It is easier to sew if you can still see through the texture to count the threads and put your needle into the surface. Fabric, ribbon or paper make for exciting extra dimensions to the preparation of an interesting background on which to stitch. Textures can be applied to the background with stitchery or bonded with a fusible webbing, following the manufacturer's instructions.

Long-armed cross variations and herringbone stitches have been worked on canvas and overlaid on ribbons machined onto the canvas. Areas were cut away to make an open grid to apply on top of another canvas.

Fabric

Netting and sheer fabrics such as organza and organdie come in an exciting range of colours and will take paint. The sheers can be torn for interesting frayed and textured edges. It is preferable to use fabric with some 'body'. Chiffons are difficult to apply well, but could be suitable for areas requiring movement or manipulation. Stitches can be sewn through the sheers to sit on the surface and contrast with the sheen. Thicker fabrics can also be manipulated and stitched in place if appropriate.

Silk fabrics bonded to the canvas will give a more solid effect on which to stitch and, although the background canvas cannot be seen, the warp and weft threads of the canvas can generally be felt through the fabric and the stitches worked as usual. It is best to keep the solid silk fabric areas small and to stitch on the edges so that the visible canvas grid can be used as a guide to stitching.

TIP

- The bonded fabric will generally stick more firmly on an interlocking canvas, simply because the background is flatter, but it works well on single canvas too with a little extra pressure and longer ironing (though take care not to singe the fabric).

In addition to the fabrics mentioned above you will be able to find paper-backed cotton, silk or organza fabric sheets, which will go through your inkjet printer to print as you would on paper. This gives you the option to print any image or take your designs from the computer onto the fabric. Once the paper backing has been peeled off the fabric, it can then be applied to your canvas.

Ribbon

Ribbons present a wonderful array of texture, pattern, width and colour from which to choose, and can easily be applied by machine, hand stitching or fusible webbing. Ribbons work well to create grids and structures on which to base a design, with the surrounding hand stitching worked to enhance and create texture. For a special effect, edges can be machine-embroidered before being appliquéd.

Paper

Papers come in very many different forms, textures and densities. Fine, delicate, decorative papers (including patterned table napkins) or specialist hand-made papers, stitched or applied to canvas with a fusible web offer another way of adding a powerful dimension to the background canvas. Small extra fibres, leaves or petals are often incorporated into the paper, which makes an interesting texture to use alongside your chosen stitches. The weight and type of paper to be used must be considered with the design.

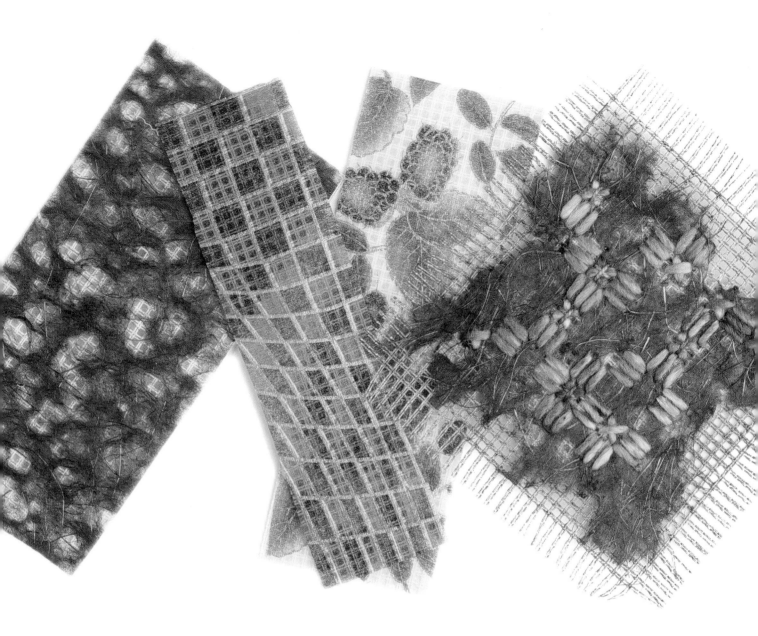

Purchased perforated papers, although more usually associated with small three-dimensional projects, can be stitched and cut to size or applied to canvas for small focal points.

Abaca tissue/Tissuetex is another useful paper, which takes paint, can be bonded or manipulated, and through which the background canvas can be seen easily for stitching.

Different types of paper bonded to canvas. The canvas holes can easily be seen through the paper for surface hand stitching.

TIP

• Once stitching has penetrated paper it cannot be taken out without leaving small holes, so take care to stitch correctly the first time around.

Silk 'paper' created from silk fibres and adhesives, although not a 'paper' in the truest sense, is wonderfully effective and rewarding for applying or bonding onto canvas as a basis for free canvas work. These papers can be highly textured with added fibres and other materials, or can be delicate with fine threads, sheer fabrics and such like trapped as the 'paper' is made. They can also be worked to incorporate canvas as the paper is being made (see also page 32).

Fusible webbing

This thin webbing of glue (which is backed onto paper) is normally used for applying fabric onto fabric, but it works well for applying fabrics or papers to canvas. As it will tear and accept paint, it can be used to give a varied colour and exciting textural finish to the surface of the background canvas.

Painted fusible webbing

The best results are achieved using thin, watered-down fabric paints or liquid paints, such as silk paints. The following are some suggestions for achieving different paint effects:

* Drop, flick or deliberately space the paint onto the fusible web with a dropper or brush, using a variety of different colours or a planned colour scheme. Lift one side of the paper vertically and the colours will run downwards in rivulets, merging together to create interesting effects and colour mixing.
* Using a sponge or medium-width paintbrush, carefully paint on your specific colours – this is more contrived and the resulting colour scheme more predictable but it may be exactly the effect you require.

After the paint has dried, you can touch up, enhance and add to your results with further over-painting using a sponge or brush. Leave the paint to dry completely before following the manufacturer's instructions to iron the web onto the canvas. Carefully peel the paper away and the painted web will be left on the canvas ready for stitching. The effects are not always predictable, which makes the final result more interesting and may well inspire an exciting embroidery as a consequence.

Painted fusible webbing can be easily applied to canvas.

Alternatively, parts of the painted webbing may be torn away from the paper and applied individually in specific areas on the canvas. Irregular shapes are formed on the canvas as the web is ironed off, and the canvas holes are easily seen through the painted web, which makes it easy to overstitch. On balance, lightly and more sensitively painted fusible webbing irons off better onto canvas and the results are more effective. When the paint is very solid or dense on the webbing, the final background effect becomes heavy and somewhat sticky.

TIPS

- Always use baking parchment underneath the canvas to be ironed and on top of the fusible webbing that you are applying, to protect the surface and iron plate.

- Take care if the painted fusible webbing is being used over large areas of canvas as it can rub off as you work. Either have extra spare pieces to iron back on or cover it carefully with tissue paper, leaving open only the area where you are stitching.

Machine stitching

On either painted or unpainted canvas, machine stitching will create its own textured background over the canvas mesh.

Machines have a wealth of patterns from which to choose, but a simple zigzag works extremely well and is a good starting point. The zigzag can be closed or open, or a selection of both, to change the look of the background canvas. Zigzags can be machined on single or double canvas. Different threads and varying colours will also alter the final effect on which to sew the canvas work stitches. Machine stitching on dissolvable papers can be applied for small areas of random texture and incorporated with canvas work stitches.

OTHER TEXTURES

There are a variety of unusual products that can be incorporated with canvas work to produce innovative and unconventional effects as a background to your stitching.

Tyvek heat-reactive fibre paper has uses from envelopes to laboratory suits, but embroiderers have discovered that it is possible to take advantage of the qualities of this paper, which change when heat is applied. This paper is available in various weights and, when heated, the plastic fibres running through the paper contract, causing interesting and distorted effects and shapes. It can be coloured or decorated before or after heating and may be applied to the background canvas for height and an interestingly raised surface. If you are going to use this raised effect in your work it is important to ensure that it merges well with your stitches to become an intrinsic part of your design.

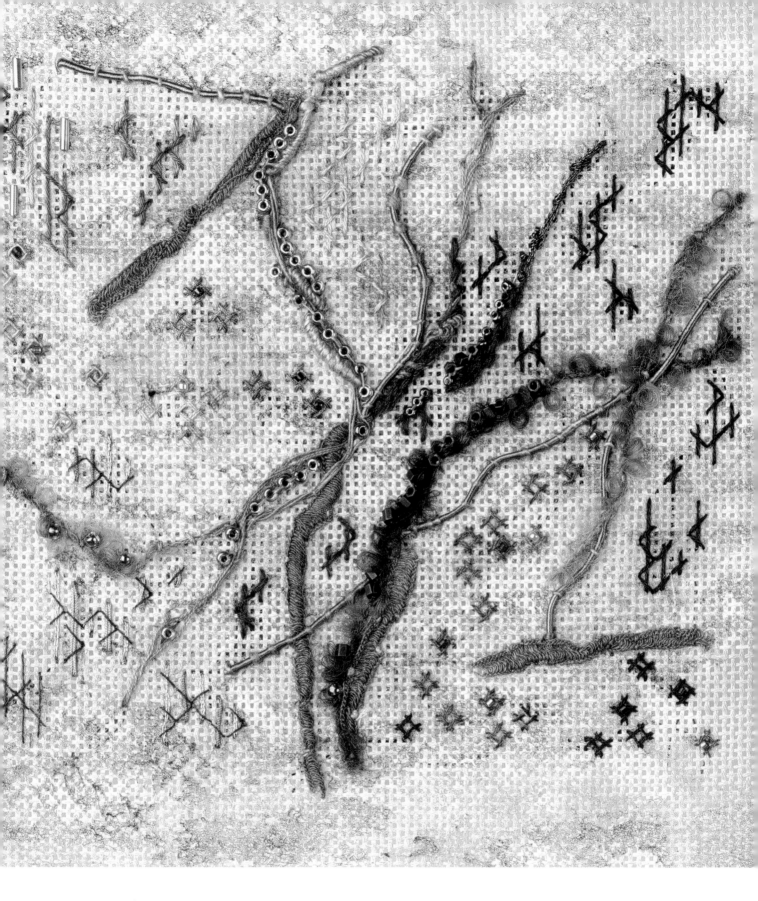

A Tissue of Contours (Ginny Evans) showing abstract laid work, between textured threads couched on canvas covered with painted fusible webbing. Beads applied with buttonhole stitch shadow the couching and there are spot motifs of braided crosses and beads.

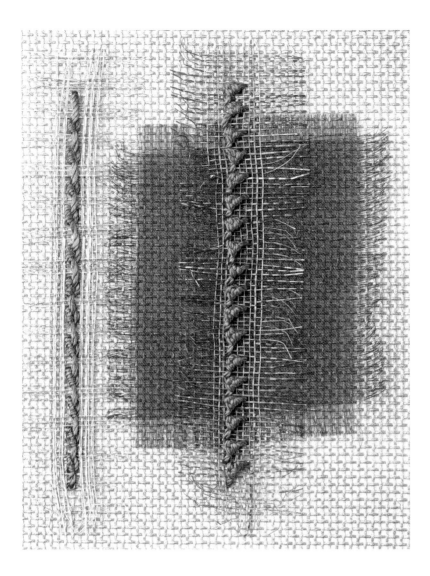

Angelina fibres are soft, lustrous fibres, which will meld together when ironed and produce bonded 'sheets' of shimmering and multicoloured effects. Like the silk 'paper' it can be layered and trapped and used with small pieces of fabric and fibres added before ironing and bonding. Angelina can be applied to canvas and the stitching worked on top or made to meander through the Angelina fibres.

Sinamai is a product or 'cloth' made of woven abaca fibres. It is currently more usually associated with fashion accessories and the millinery trade, and is found in a variety of weaves – some with a definite open grid and others with an uneven open weave, both of which make an interesting texture to apply to canvas and overstitch. Sinamai 'cloth' can be purchased in lengths or in ribbon widths. It handles well applied to canvas, will take colour and can be further stiffened with PVA if necessary.

Sizoflor, a 'paper' of abaca fibres meshed together, is exceptionally useful and suitable for bonding and applying onto canvas. This alternative 'paper', which is fine and delicate enough to see and stitch through onto the canvas ground, does not break down when stitched and takes colour well. It does not tear freely like some hand-made papers, but does come in a wide range of colours and can be found in lengths or ribbon widths.

Sheers and sinamai applied to canvas with palestrina knot and double knot embroidery stitches.

Sample (Ginny Evans) using simple couching to secure the textured novelty wool on painted fusible webbing applied to canvas.

Wire comes in all manner of meshes, lengths and thicknesses suitable for stitching on and incorporating with canvas work. Specialist wire companies will sell small, manageable pieces or longer lengths. A shape cut out of the canvas ground could be filled with a wire mesh 'slip' especially easily, as the wire mesh does not fray. This is all the more effective if the wire mesh and canvas background are of different size count.

Iridescent acetate is a captivating source of glistening opalescence, which reflects all manner of colours. It is fairly strong and flexible and can be shaped, stitched or melted with a hot air tool. The shimmering effect can be overpowering, so it is advisable to show some restraint when incorporating it into your work!

Arti stick paints can be used straight from the tube, squeezed onto glass or plastic for shape or line. After 24 hours, once the paint has dried, it can be lifted off the surface and repositioned on the background canvas. It dries smooth, so could be used for highlighting or definition.

3 Colour, design and stitch

COLOUR

Colour preferences and combinations are very personal means of self-expression and, subconsciously, colours can significantly reflect or influence our moods. Planning and working satisfactorily with colour does not come easily to everyone, as colour theories can be highly academic and complex. As embroiderers we would like to have a good working knowledge of the colour spectrum to provide a basis for the understanding of relationships in colour and use of tones to give individuality and life to our work. Many of us play safe with our colour schemes and prefer to follow similar colour choices to our clothing or interiors, with which we already feel comfortable. We all have our favourites, so this is the moment to break out, face the challenge and experiment with colours not normally used and invigorate your embroidery.

To give you confidence, collect cards, pictures from magazines/brochures, fabrics, photographs etc., where the colour schemes appeal to you. In addition to observing colour around you, create your own notebook of colour schemes with collages of thread, fabric, paper and your favourite colouring method. This will make you focus positively to develop your own understanding and appreciation of colour. Analyse why the scheme is successful and make notes as to why you like it.

Understanding the fundamental principles of the colour wheel and perceiving the relationships of colour is a good starting point. See the spectrum in a range of pure colour based on the three primary colours:

- The primary colours of red, blue and yellow cannot be mixed from any other colour.
- The secondary colours of orange, green and violet are produced by mixing two primaries together. i.e. red and yellow for orange, yellow and blue for green, blue and red for violet.
- The tertiary colours are produced by mixing one primary and one secondary together, i.e. red-orange, yellow-orange, yellow-green, blue-green, blue-violet and red-violet; or mixing the secondary colours together, i.e. green and violet to make olive.

Colour definitions make it easier to make sense of the theories as follows:

- **Hue** is another word for colour.
- **Tone** is the degree of difference in the intensity of a colour.
- **Value** is the lightness or darkness of a hue (colour).
- **Tint** is the pure colour combined with white to produce a lighter tone of a hue.
- **Shade** is the pure colour combined with black to produce a darker tone of a hue.
- **Saturation** is the intensity of colour free from any addition of white or black.

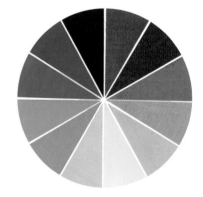

Above
Refer to the colour wheel to help you plan successful colour schemes.

Right
Use your own photographs to create a colour palette and observe texture.

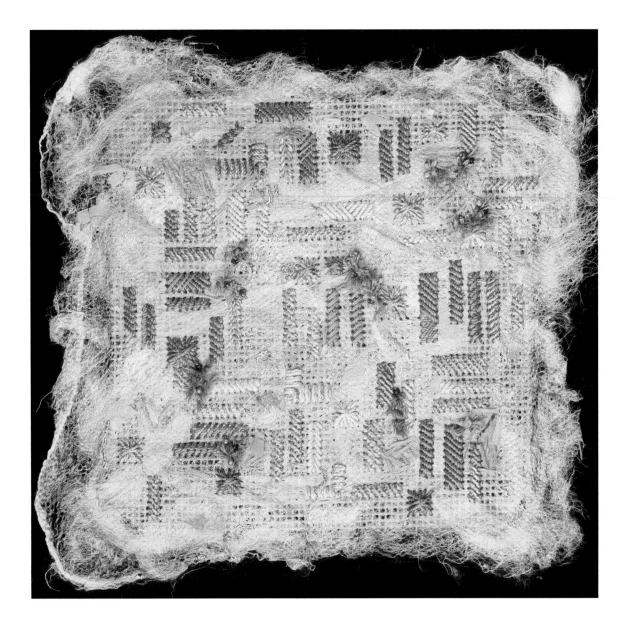

From the colour palette, decide on a colour scheme referring to the colour wheel as follows:

- **Achromatic colour scheme** is a colourless scheme that uses blacks, whites and greys.
- **Monochromatic colour scheme** uses the tones, tints and shades of one colour. Tonal variation and use of each tint or shade will govern the success of this scheme.
- **Split complementary scheme** is selecting one colour and using the colours each side of its complement on the colour wheel, e.g. red with blue-green and yellow-green.
- **Complementary colour scheme** uses colours that lie opposite to each other on the colour wheel, e.g. red/green, yellow/violet, blue/orange.
- **Triadic colour scheme** uses a rich harmony of three colours equidistant from each other for balance and symmetry, e.g. red, yellow and blue, violet, orange and green.
- **Analogous colour scheme** uses the tones, tints and shades of two to four colours that are adjacent to each other on the wheel, e.g. blue/green/yellow. Harmony occurs, by association, with colours in which the same primary is incorporated.

Colour schemes must always be considered with their setting and use planned in advance. The correct tonal value, proportions and areas of colour are crucial for a successful colour scheme.

The Aftermath – Hurricane Katrina (Jill Carter) shows an assortment of textures incorporated into hand-made silk 'paper', which was overlaid onto canvas and stitched with satin, Rhodes, knitting and Ghiordes knot.

TIPS

- Adding a contrast will serve to vitalize a colour scheme.

- Warm colours are the reds, oranges and sunny yellows.

- Cool colours are the greens, blues and violets.

- Neutral colours are made up of combinations of black and white.

COLOUR AND STITCH

The fun and challenges come when you look for your colours in thread and thread textures as colour associations are the link between your design and stitching. When choosing your colours for embroidery, start with your main colour and follow with your secondary colours, remembering to incorporate varying tones and considering each for its value to captivate and add something to the scheme. Bringing in other elements to perform in the colour scheme, such as beads, will need to be evaluated carefully at the planning stage and not added as an afterthought – as well as colour they bring significant variations of texture. Colours change dramatically or blend together depending on which ones are placed in conjunction with each other, and stitching on a coloured background will bring additional factors that must be taken into consideration. For instance, if the ground colour is green and the stitching is blue and executed so that the green ground shows through the stitching, the colours will merge to produce a blue-green effect. Likewise blending colours using stitches works if there are two or more journeys forming the stitch, such as a rice stitch or double straight cross, as colours can be combined in contrasting ways on the different journeys.

Harmonious colour scheme sample (Ginny Evans) on a transfer-painted background with contrasting smooth and textured canvas stitches including cushion variation, tent, long-armed cross, tied oblong cross and arrowhead.

DESIGN

The fundamentals of design comprise line, shape, form, colour, texture and pattern, and all these elements will be involved in developing designs for your canvas work embroidery.

Communicating with line is the ideal starting point, and to get off the ground you need go no further than bar codes as a source of inspiration. Nothing could be a more plentiful or unthreatening source of design than the different width of lines established on bar codes – found on most items in your store cupboard.

Look for an interesting bar code with unevenly spaced narrow and wide, black and white lines and already we are into the element of shape.

Before translating your lines into stitch and pattern, work through the design exercise on page 36 to help you understand the effects created by counter-changing the bands, by introducing and counter-changing pattern to develop spatial awareness.

Computer-generated bar code and bar code sample in black and white satin stitches to demonstrate the effects of different widths of line using contrasts, e.g. the wide bands of white stitching are more prominent than the wide bands of black stitching.

Exploring colour in bands

Above

Bar code sample in a contrasting colour scheme showing transfer-painted background and applied sizoflor with textured canvas stitches – long-armed cross reversed tent, woven, double. This is a good way of practising colour mixing and combinations of colour, stitch, thread and texture.

Left

Expanding the bar code theme to find inspiration and pattern in everyday life for developing into a design for your canvas work.

Using paints or water-based pencils/crayons and following the bar code concept, explore different colour schemes by experimenting and painting your own bands of colour and colour combinations. Try painting on dry paper and then slightly dampen a page of the sketchbook and repeat the process. The paints will run together to create different shades and tones.

Working samples with an uncomplicated and elementary design source such as a bar code is a good way to develop basic design skills, reinforce your study of colour, and find out about texture in stitch and thread. Making samples and keeping notes are an invaluable part of the learning process, and there is a lot of satisfaction in turning the samples into a stimulating and spectacular portfolio for future reference. If you are experienced, you can enjoy the challenge of experimenting with colour and discovering a new set of stitches you have not used before.

Progressing your skills

From simple beginnings you will be able to move on and embark on a more adventurous journey to develop your designing skills and create a less formalized or abstract pattern with your bar codes.

Experimenting with the following exercises will help you develop your own designs for stitching.

- Take different sized photocopies of the bar codes, and cut into strips of different widths and lengths. Form squares with some of the stripes to create focal points.
- Try 'exploding' them apart to give you some spaces, or turn sideways, intersect, weave or angle the different widths of strips to develop the design (see also page 39).
- Introduce a colour scheme with coloured plain or patterned papers instead of the black and white bars. Emphasize and create focal points with your coloured papers. Once you are satisfied, stick them into position and get ready to portray your design with stitch (see **Introducing colour** on page 35).

Looking around for more ambitious subject matters from which to design, you will be surprised to find how many examples relate to the bar code theme. Inspiration and pattern is everywhere – to investigate, exploit and develop for your own ends (see photographs on pages 31 and 34).

Above left
Develop the bar code into a simple design.

Above right
Further develop the bar code into a grid design.

Right
Moving on with Bar Codes (Gillian Bray) showing a transfer-painted background, with painted fusible webbing texture and paper appliqué. Laid patterns are included with cushion stitches, double tied oblong cross, Hungarian, braided cross, satin and tent stitch.

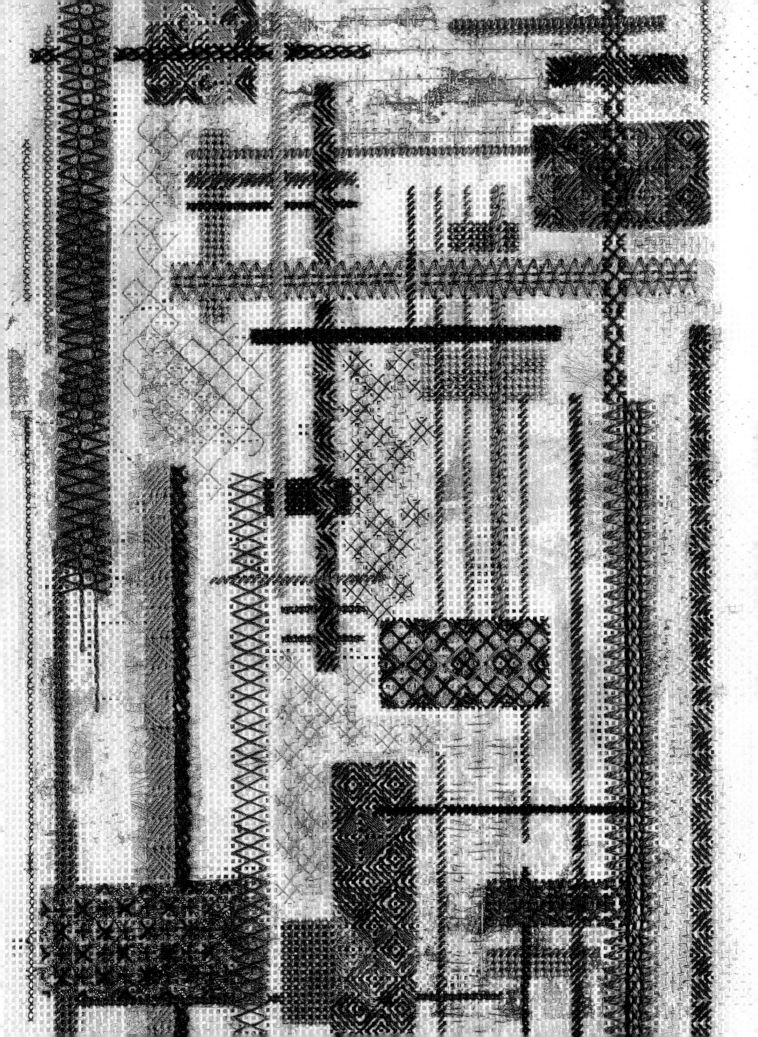

Repeating patterns

Geometric patterns, grids of squares, rectangles and triangles (often found on floors and walls of ancient buildings) are an endless source of repeating patterns to use in canvas work. They can be translated onto squared paper, cut out, developed and used as a reference point to create further patterns. Alternatively, a specific shape can be manipulated in a variety of ways to create a repeating pattern – a number of copies made and lined up beside each other, half dropped or reversed. Combining different dimensions of the shape will produce a new image with new contours to work with and explore.

Using a computer to develop your own designs is an exciting way of shortening or expanding some of the usual designing processes. If you feel confident on the computer, there is no reason not to embrace and experiment with the powerful elements of design that the computer will offer you. Even if your skills and understanding of the computer are limited, with a little practice you will soon be able to master relatively basic skills, such as selecting a part of a sketch or design, juxtaposing, reversing or multiplying it, to create your own images for embroidery that will undoubtedly lead to yet more inspiration and ideas.

Sketch of a datura flower.

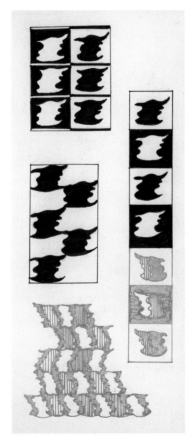

Developing elements of the datura into repeat negative and positive patterns for a final design. This could be further developed into an all-over pattern for a cushion, for example (see embroidery on page 97).

Sketch book page developing the
bar code theme – exploding
different widths of strips and
forming grids.

Left
Developing elements on the
computer from the datura sketch
for a repeating pattern. Interpret
the final design on canvas with
free cable stitch outline, Jessica
and eyelet circles with random
laid pattern fillings.

STITCH

The stitch repertoire for canvas work is open-ended and wonderfully inspiring, as there are so many alternatives, variations and combinations to be considered. In addition, not only can the embroiderer draw upon stitches specifically for canvas work, but also on embroidery stitches and other counted-thread techniques that combine well on canvas.

Experimenting and making the choice for a given piece of work is the immense fun and challenge of canvas work. Small or large, flat or raised, open or solid, combinations or patterns developed from the basics all give the stitcher prodigious scope for a really interesting interpretation of any design. Contrasting textures of stitch with thread (rough and smooth, matt and shiny) to exploit the play of light will add additional dimension to the piece.

As with any skill, experimenting and working samples prior to starting a major piece will probably save many hours of angst and unpicking. Continue to use the bar code idea for samples not only for exploring colour schemes and practising different background textures, but also for learning and incorporating your chosen range of stitches.

To develop the bar codes into a design for stitch, imagine the width of these bars represent a number of canvas threads and give each bar a hypothetical number from 1 to 6 depending on the breadth of each bar. These can be translated into threads of the canvas so that you can choose stitches that will work vertically over one thread, over two threads, over three, four, five or six threads. Select stitches that you already know or use the stitches listed below to get you started. Keep it simple to begin with, but remember that stitches may be developed and expanded and worked to create further patterns.

Your samples can be as deep or as wide as you wish. To begin with, set limitations of colour and stitch and restrict yourself to a light and dark colour (imitating the black and white bar stripes) with a range of no more than three or four stitches, such as two smooth and two textured, and gradually build up to more complex combinations. Study your sample so that you can evaluate the resulting effect of this basic exercise in balance. Spatial balances and effects are considerations that you will need to establish when translating colour and stitch into your designs.

The look and the effect of the canvas work stitches changes according to the size of canvas and thickness of thread being used – whether you intend to cover the canvas or whether you intend to expose the canvas. Contemporary canvas works well when both alternatives are used.

There are so many stitches to discover that will depict anything you want and, although there will always be favourites, it is well worth researching and investigating new ones and trying them out.

The stitches on page 42 have been selected specifically because the individual unit is worked over a particular number of vertical canvas threads and is appropriate for the bar code theme. Some are textured and some smooth. When the stitches are repeated or added to, they will develop into other patterns and become available to use over different numberings.

Bag 'Hanging' (Jill Carter): spray-painted canvas with cushion, Leviathan and mosaic stitches bordered by mesa stitch. Hand-twisted cord with simple tassels.

Stitch Suggestions

Stitches worked over one vertical thread
- Tent (continental)
- Double
- Tied oblong cross

Stitches worked over two vertical threads
- Vandyke
- Cashmere
- Kalem
- Mosaic

Stitches worked over three vertical threads
- Satin (Gobelin)
- Long and short oblique
- Fern
- Wheat

Stitches worked over four vertical threads
- Interlaced cross
- Double leviathan
- Arrowhead
- Algerian eye

Stitches worked over five vertical threads
- Double tied oblong cross (sideways)
- Butterfly
- Wild goose chase
- Half Rhodes

Stitches worked over six vertical threads
- Eyelets
- Windmill
- Beaty

Stitches of varying dimensions
- Cushion (Scotch) stitch over three to five

5 threads
- Diagonal Gobelin stitch (satin stitch) over two or more threads
- Smyrna cross over two and four threads
- Rice over two and four threads
- Long-armed cross over two or more threads

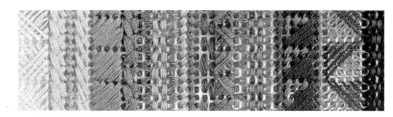

Cushion variation, tent, long-armed cross, tied oblong cross and arrowhead

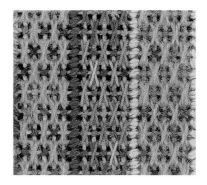

Double

Cushion

Interlaced cross

Windmill

Eyelet

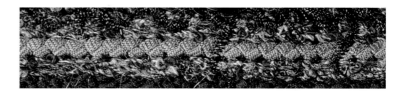

Long-armed cross

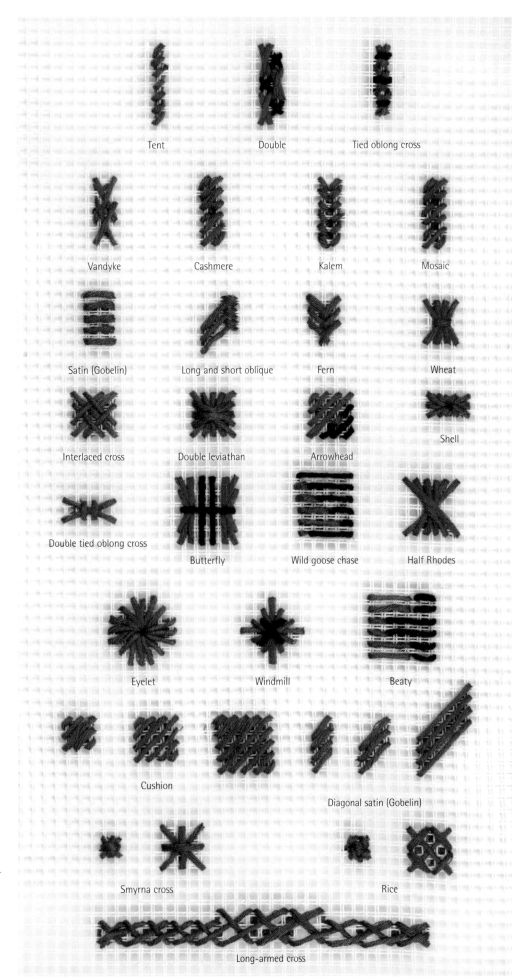

Tent   Double   Tied oblong cross

Vandyke   Cashmere   Kalem   Mosaic

Satin (Gobelin)   Long and short oblique   Fern   Wheat

Interlaced cross   Double leviathan   Arrowhead   Shell

Double tied oblong cross   Butterfly   Wild goose chase   Half Rhodes

Eyelet   Windmill   Beaty

Cushion   Diagonal satin (Gobelin)

Smyrna cross   Rice

Long-armed cross

Overleaf
Work the stitches in the sampler (right), following the diagrams on pages 44-45. Bring your needle up at 1, go down at 2, up at 3 and so on.

Stitches

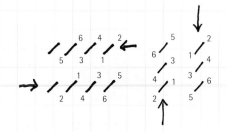

Tent

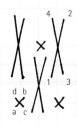

Double

Tied oblong cross

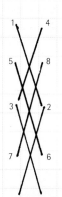

Vandyke

Cashmere

Kalem

Mosaic

Satin (Gobelin)

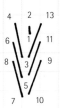

Long and short oblique

Fern

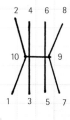

Wheat

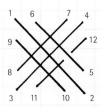

Interlaced cross

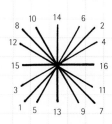

Double leviathan

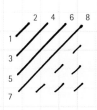

Arrowhead

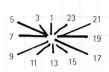

Algerian eye

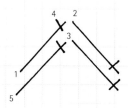

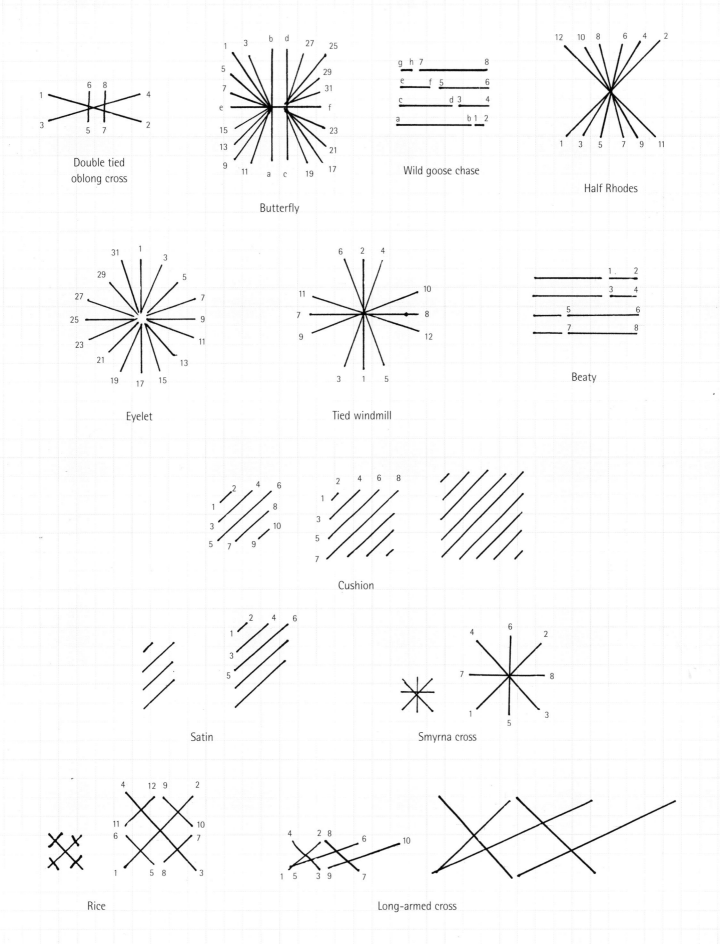

Double tied
oblong cross

Butterfly

Wild goose chase

Half Rhodes

Eyelet

Tied windmill

Beaty

Cushion

Satin

Smyrna cross

Rice

Long-armed cross

4 Couching on a canvas background

Familiarly associated with the laid patterns of crewel work or gold work embroidery techniques, simple line couching will also be found on textiles throughout the world in one form or another. Couching easily makes the transition to canvas work and it is an invaluable technique to use in conjunction with the usual canvas work stitches, for defining, creating curves, following more intricate designs, outlining or infilling, and accentuating. Threads which would be difficult to sew in the usual way suddenly become viable when couched as surface decoration.

The term couching generally refers to the stitching down of a thread on the surface of a background fabric, following a shape or design, and relates to a thread which cannot be taken through the ground fabric. However, threads may also be laid and couched down to fill areas with decorative or shaded patterns.

In their simplest, most traditional form, arrangements of small straight stitches (formed at right angles to the couched thread) are stitched over the surface thread. These small stitches, which tie down the surface thread, can be evenly spaced, lined up to form brick patterns or placed at random. Spacing is dependent on the design and preference. Stitches or groups of stitches can be considered as an integral part of the design or they are merely a means of containing the surface thread as invisibly as possible.

Other couching techniques such as Bokhara and Roumanian differ from traditional methods in that only one needle and thread is used. The couching thread is taken across the background fabric and is fastened down on the return journey with the same needle and thread, in the case of Bokhara with short slanting stitches and in the case of Roumanian with long slanting stitches.

Used in conjunction with an even-weave canvas background, the ever-increasing range of glorious threads and textured yarns present all manner of possibilities for achieving interesting couched designs and textures. The geometric nature of canvas work stitches and designs can be softened or shaped with thick or thin couching. Line and form become anything you want.

Couching Sampler (Juliet Pollard) showing a wide range of canvas and embroidery stitches that can be used for couching metallics/fibres onto a canvas background.

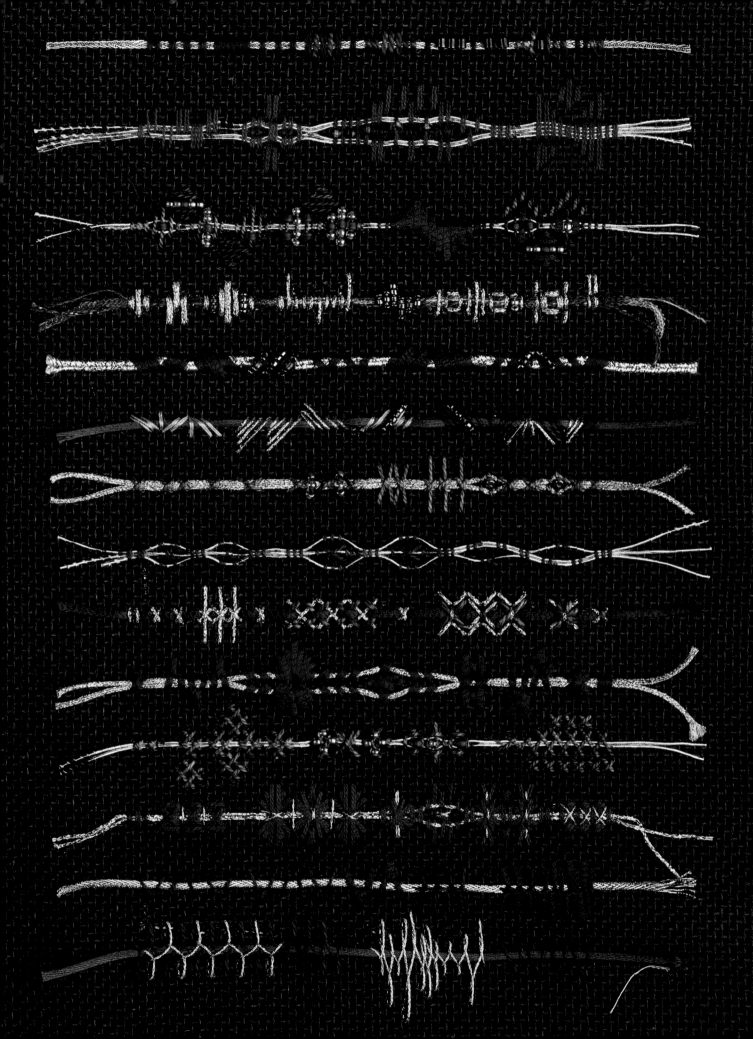

COUCHING WITH CANVAS WORK STITCHES

Surface threads of any texture and dimension may be stitched down with a wide choice of possible canvas work stitches. Stitches can be developed to infill formal patterns or to achieve free and more fluid interpretations of a design, using a variety of threads or incorporating beads.

- Straight stitch couching could include stitches such as brick (satin), Gobelin, Parisian, Hungarian, pavilion and their many variations.
- Couching with diagonal stitches could encompass tent, slanted Gobelin, kalem, diagonal mosaic, variations of cushion (Scotch) or Moorish.
- Couching with textured stitches could incorporate variations and combinations of cross stitches such as rice, double-tied oblong, half Rhodes.
- Double lines of couching will work well with wheat, shell stitch or fly stitch.

COUCHING WITH EMBROIDERY STITCHES

Using decorative embroidery stitches such as the cross, chain and herringbone families opens up yet more choices to add another dimension and texture to couching but should be used within the context of the canvas work.

- Stitches such as lock, fly, thorn, crown, loop, and Cretan also lend themselves to couching, and work effectively on canvas and with canvas stitches for a creative abstract effect.

COUCHING WITH BEADS

Cords couched down with beads is a unique way of creating lines of texture, height and variety in your canvas work. Anchor the string securely on to the canvas using normal sewing thread and a sharp needle and alternating from side to side, take small evenly spaced stab stitches through the cord. Ensure that you have enough beads on your thread to cover and sit over the cord. Varying the size and type of bead will further raise the surface on your canvas.

LAID FILLINGS

Couching takes on a different life with laid fillings when the evenweave mesh of canvas can be fully exploited with the symmetry of the surface patterns. Laid fillings, more often associated with silk, crewel or gold work embroidery, give the embroiderer a wealth of designs from the simple to the complex to use on canvas either for filling a designated shape, for using as a background or simply for another texture.

Laid patterns open up all sorts of opportunities for employing exciting or subtle colour schemes, shadowing and shading. The combinations are endless, as are the patterns which can be worked densely or with fine threads for a more open effect where the ground canvas is exposed and becomes an integral part of the final impression.

Pineapple (Juliet Pollard) showing four-way Continental stitch and a variety of laid patterns using shaded cotton threads and overlaid with crescents.

Details shown below right.

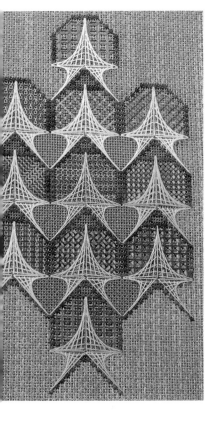

Long 'trammed' threads/stitches are the basis of laid patterns which are characteristically formed with a length of thread going across from one side of the area being filled to the other. Keep the canvas as taut as possible so that the long threads are set straight. The framework of threads can be laid horizontally, vertically, or diagonally and formed to make single lines, a trellis of vertical and horizontal lines (into either squares or diamond shapes), or worked with more complex combinations of all three. Working the foundation threads back and forth will save thread, as the linking thread lies down the sides of the area being worked and, in addition, there are no bulky or unsightly threads intruding from the back of the work. This is essential if working an open filling where any coloured threads crossing on the back would show through to the front. The starting and finishing thread can be worked in or attached to the sides of the design.

When the basic foundation is laid, the long threads are tied/couched in place with a variety of stitches from tent/obliques, straight, crosses, to the more complex and decorative stitch combinations. The closer the foundation lines are positioned the more dense the effect, generally resulting in space for only simple tying stitches. With the framework distanced wider apart, the effect will be lighter and there will be more space for either a combination of tying stitches, or extra embellishment.

Tying stitches can be made in simple bricking formations as seen in the familiar Burden stitch, or developed with multiple combinations to create additional patterns or bolder arrangements. Keeping an even tension is important when a number of stitches have to be made into the same hole.

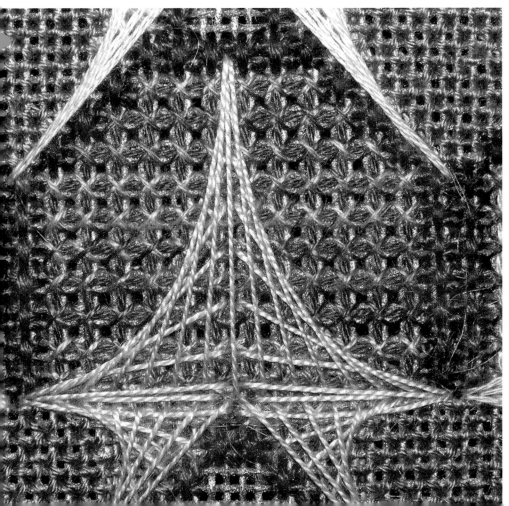

CREATIVE IDEAS

The effect achieved with laid patterns is governed by the choice of thread and the fantastic array of different threads now available will help you accomplish anything you wish. Experimenting with threads and patterns is an important part of understanding the myriad effects of laid patterns and well worth undertaking – any samples can go into your portfolio for future reference where they will not be wasted, so consider some of the following:

- The same pattern may be varied enormously with changes of colour, texture and weight of the threads and can be an exciting contrast against the usual canvas work stitches.
- Delicate, fine threads can give just a hint of texture in a background while thicker threads may work better for a filling.
- Use laying and couching threads of a similar colour to emphasize and strengthen the pattern.
- Combine several different thicknesses of thread where the laid filling is more complex and has a number of stages, always keeping the thicker threads for the laying and the finer threads for the couching.
- Use fillings to 'couch' down paper or other such materials for a fresh approach.
- Incorporate twigs, hand-made wire beads, pipe cleaners as part of the laid grid for a more significant textured effect.

Right
Jungle Business (Helen Lewis) shows leather covering a thick padding, and a variety of cords and textured threads couched randomly for a 2-D effect onto a painted background. Unpadded leather and stitch shading shapes the tiger. Embroidery stitches – fly, long and short – are combined with tent and leaf canvas work stitches for texture.

Left
Estuary (Mary Pinch) showing cords and string couched with straight and crown stitches interspersed with abstract laid work on a sprayed and partially painted background.

5 Embroidery stitches on canvas

Embroidery stitches open a gamut of spectacular choices to include with canvas work embroidery and will provide you with yet more scope for enhancing your design. A whole new world of depicting texture, line and shape presents itself for embellishing and incorporating with canvas stitches. Changing the dimensions of the stitches will afford a contemporary interpretation of the traditional.

Forming curves can so often prove problematical within the confines of a design on a geometric grid but embroidery stitches will usually provide the solution as well as being an excellent substitute for couching and will comfortably integrate with canvas stitches.

Representational canvas work (as opposed to abstract designs) is greatly enhanced when embroidery and canvas work stitches are combined. Intermixing the two techniques on canvas will present you with opportunities for a more fluid interpretation of your design and where appropriate will help to make the canvas work appear less rigid and geometric, as well as creating depth and individuality in the finished piece.

LINE STITCHES

Simple line stitches are the basis of embroidery. These basic stitches are satisfyingly straightforward to work and, depending on the stitch and thread being used, will create wide or narrow lines as wished or infill a design. They are important for emphasis and convenient for the shadowing of either straight or curved lines. The most familiar of the line stitches are backstitch, stem, split and the variations of chain.

Back, stem or split stitch can be exploited for texture on tree bark, sky or water. Stitches may be lined up closely in bands or elongated to fit the circumstances. Split stitch in fine silks will enable you to create perfect shading on flower petals, leaves or animals and may be executed to follow curved outlines and shapes.

Shell Structure (Jill Carter) shows a painted fusible webbing background with free straight stitch machining texture. Palestrina, French and double knot embroidery stitches with simple couching outline the design of applied leather with reversed tent and mosaic, random double stitch, and braided cross. Free machining granite stitch has been worked throughout the design for unity.

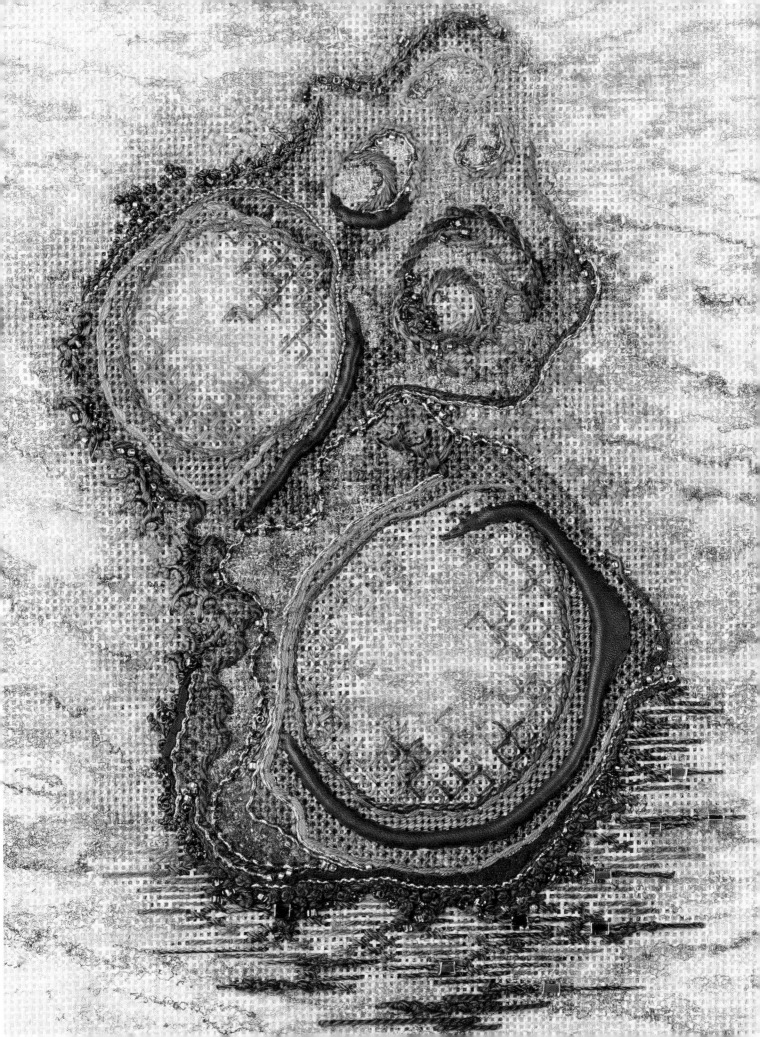

The variations of **chain stitches** – open, twisted, whipped or knotted – offer a range of possibilities for line and pattern. Working in varying lengths or in a diversity of threads gives the chain stitches a contemporary feel and opens the door to freedom of movement either in lines or packed up closely in a given shape. Smaller stitches may be made within larger ones for added effect.

Buttonhole stitch is a wonderfully expressive and decorative line stitch, which will work in the round, as a line, or wrapped for emphasis, and is particularly effective when stitched close together with varying lengths of stitch for randomly infilling areas of a design.

Cretan stitch dramatically widens the field for interpreting lines and is a very useful stitch to master. Worked freely it will 'flow' for water, stand upright for grass, indicate shape and outline on a horizon, move upwards or sideways for contours, or it can be superimposed on top of other stitches for another dimension. Thread variations will enhance the stitch and influence the resulting final outcome.

KNOTTED LINE STITCHES

Knotted line stitches provide more scope for added character and texture, particularly when stitched freely and in different sizes. Stitches such as Palestrina knot, double knot, knotted loop or Portuguese knotted stem are great fun to do, especially worked in varying thicknesses of thread, and are useful for creating height and depth against flatter canvas work stitches. These softer knotted and textured line stitches make an excellent foil for the geometric nature of the technique and, with the qualities of the background canvas, it is easy to keep the stitches any size you wish.

The Palestrina and double knot can be produced simply in lines, enlarged with more than one knot/stitch formed on each bar, worked in different directions or formed with uneven length stitches. Packed into bands beside smoother canvas stitches, the knot stitches are an interesting variation of texture.

Knotted stitches and textured threads combined with canvas work stitches will also provide an intriguing background surface on which to machine either freely or using the decorative patterns available on your sewing machine.

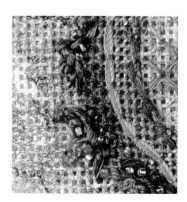

Right
Bag (Jill Carter) with bands of stem, palestrina, double knot and long-armed cross stitches that were worked in wools, ribbon and textured yarns and overstitched with a decorative machine pattern. Wrapped rings form the handles with simple tassels attached with painted paper clips.

INDIVIDUAL STITCHES

Useful detached embroidery stitches such as seeding, chain or fly will fill in a background to give depth or a basis for further overstitching. Individual stitches may be built up densely and will create wonderful textures for greenery and leaves, making it easy to give the impression of shadows and distance.

Simple **seeding or spotting stitches** offer scope for delicately filled shapes, working as contrast to solid canvas stitches.

Utilitarian **detached chain stitches** will not only encompass flower petals, but can be stitched in all directions in different proportions to create textural variations or can enclose other stitches such as a bullion knot. Larger chain stitches can be infilled with smaller ones, with a change of thread or colour to broaden the horizons of the individual stitch.

Detached chain stitches

Fly stitch can be treated in a similar way to chain stitches and will afford just as satisfying results. It can be lined up neatly for leaves, stitched randomly in any direction to cover the background or worked individually as a single detail. The dimension of the stitch can be significantly changed by the angle at which the needle is inserted into the background. It can be elongated or shortened, overstitched with a second fly stitch or finished off with a long or short 'tail'.

Knots

The individual surface stitches of the knot family, such as French, bullion or raised are invaluable for applying virtually anywhere. They can be 'spotted' to provide speckles or areas of colour and used with a wide range of different threads for contrast or texture, presenting endless possibilities for integrating embroidery stitches with canvas work. Beads can be included with the knots to glisten and shimmer.

French knots

French knots can be enlarged with thicker thread or reduced with thinner thread, but should have just one wrap on the needle so that the construction of the knot is not lost. Relevant to the composition of a design, they can be packed tightly into areas for substance and infilling, formed loosely to leave loops of thread or worked over stitches already established for a more raised surface. Impressions of flowers on a stalk, or texture and shade in water can be created with a long stitch finishing off the knot instead of the thread being tucked in neatly beside the starting point as usual.

Bullion knots, being more bulky and obvious, used creatively, bring additional emphasis and lift to a piece of embroidery. They can be treated in the same manner as French knots and can be extremely chunky or very delicate, as necessary. The best effects are achieved using a single twist thread with the number of wraps equating to the length of stitch taken. The stitch can also be formed to make curves by overwrapping, elongated with 'tails', stacked side by side for added texture, enclosed with other stitches such as chain or fly, arranged in patterns or flower shapes, or simply used to couch.

Bullion knots

Raised knots are worked individually on a cross-stitch foundation, with a backstitch worked round the cross stitch to cover each 'arm' of the cross. As with the French and bullion knots, the colour and texture of thread will determine the final effect.

The Burden stitch background is overstitched with close zigzag machining. The flower petals are made up of free straight stitch machining, bullion knots and detached chain with French knots for the centre.

COMPOSITE STITCHES

Composite stitches, such as those worked on a foundation or with a combination of stitches/journeys, will help you tackle the requirement for thick bands, wider curves or borders.

Stitches such as **raised stem** or **chain bands** are worked on a foundation ladder, which can be formed close together or wide apart. The stem or chain on the foundation ladder can be evenly or randomly spaced, narrowed and widened, worked freely, wrapped and further transformed by the choice of thread. Owing to its nature the stitch will work in abstract pieces as well as representational ones, where it could be used for trees, paths, fields or even a roof.

TIP

- An alternative effect when you are creating lines of raised stem or chain bands is to abandon the foundation ladder and work the stitches directly onto the canvas grid (see opposite).

Serpentine or **threaded backstitch**, which is also a line stitch, is very effective worked in different colours and types of thread. It works well as a filling stitch, and very successfully straight or on the diagonal to divide up or outline a design. On canvas, if the threaded stitch is worked in a single twist and pulled up tightly, the resulting effect is a raised ridge.

CREATIVE IDEAS

- Use contrasting threads, different thicknesses or shimmering metallics to accentuate or highlight stitches.
- Simple stitches such as fly or shisha make an interesting overstitch on top of canvas work stitches for an added decorative effect and to draw attention to the textures.
- 'Whipping' or wrapping the stitches will further decorate or raise the texture as appropriate to the design, the end result being dominated by the choice of thread and how many times the stitches have been wrapped.
- Liven up areas of matt stitching with glistening beads, if appropriate, to give some relevance to the design.

Right

Stitch, Paper and Plastic (Jill Carter) combines embroidery stitches with canvas work stitches using a variety of threads. Withdrawn threads create a foundation for raised chain band; Gobelin and squared herringbone secure paper rectangles; Roumanian couching was used to apply the straw hinges; cushion stitches, which divide the applied straws and double knot stitch, are overstitched with fly.

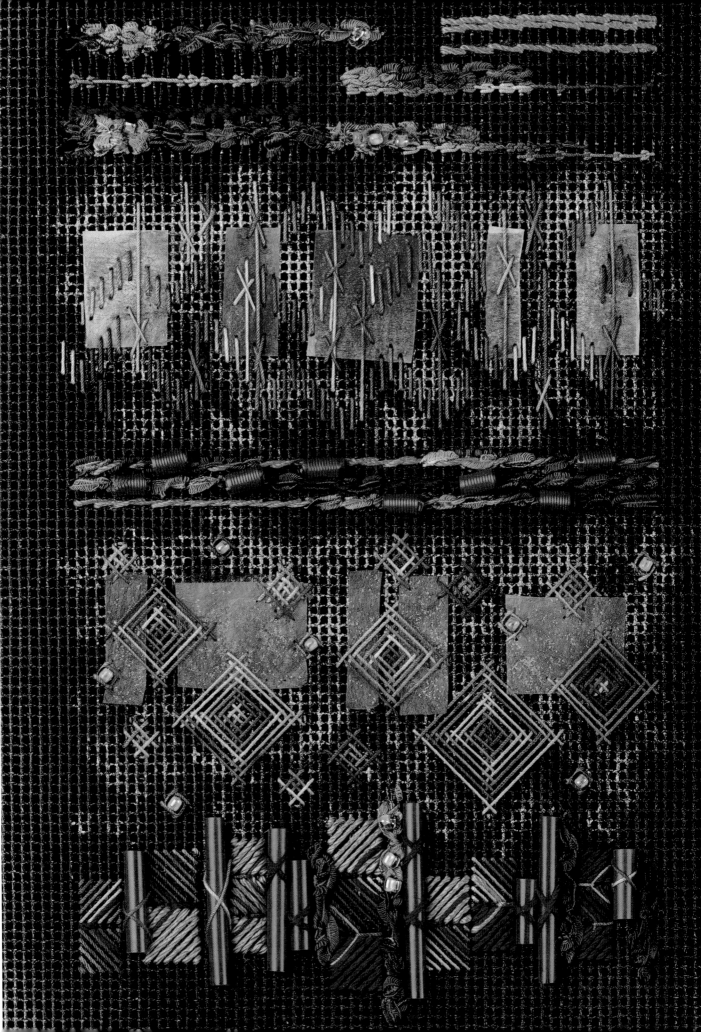

6 Applying objects onto a canvas background

Within the context of your design you can successfully apply all manner of items onto canvas to intermingle with canvas stitches. Applying items opens up a powerful opportunity to enhance or develop canvas work in a more abstract way. How to apply the objects either comes in the category of being couched or requiring decorative stitching.

A piece of work with applied objects (apart, perhaps, from small beads) is not usually something that will stand lots of wear and tear, and is generally more suitable for a wall panel or conversation piece. These factors should be considered before embarking on your masterpiece.

Background canvas work stitches can enhance, complement, contrast or simply be unobtrusive. Determining the colour and thickness of the thread is the key to achieving the result you are looking for. Stitches such as Alicia's lace, reversed cushion (Scotch), brick, simple laid patterns or darning stitches in fine threads will produce a light all-over effect. More dominant effects will result if the thread is thicker or more substantial stitches are used such as brick, rice, Milanese, oriental, cashmere, mosaic, or cushion (Scotch) (see page 68).

LEATHER

Leather, either padded, unpadded or manipulated, is a very effective medium for creating smooth contrasts, texture or emphasis against canvas stitches. It is generally possible to use either the rough or smooth side of the leather to maximize the textures and, apart from being used for incorporating into abstract designs, leather is convenient for representing bark, rocks/strata or buildings and architecture.

For padding leather, felt or string may be applied to the canvas. The pieces of felt or string should be cut to size and stab stitched into place with small stitches to secure it onto the canvas. If you are applying more than one layer of padding, the first layer should be smaller than subsequent layers. Lay the leather over the padding and imprint the outline with a sharp needle. Cut the leather on the imprint line and stab stitch with small, evenly spaced stitches, close to the edge.

Manipulated leather requires leather cut larger than the area you are going to cover. Either stitch the leather down on one side of the given shape and manoeuvre it into place, securing the folds and creases with small backstitches; or stitch round the entire piece within the given shape, manipulate and stitch the slack into position.

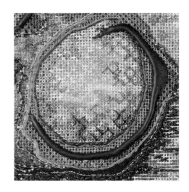

Close-up of leather detail from *Shell Structure* on page 53.

Heraldic Leopard 'Supporter' (Jill Carter)
using traditional canvas work stitches
combined with embroidery and metal
thread techniques and leather
application on a painted background.

TIPS

- Pay particular attention to your technique when you are stitching down the padding. If it has been applied badly, it will be reflected in the finished appearance of the leather.

- Leather may be cut into any shape or have holes punched out of it for further interest.

MIRRORS, COINS, METAL SHIM AND MESH

There are a variety of canvas stitches appropriate for applying mirrors, metal shims and meshes to the background canvas. Making the right choice means the applied objects become important either as a focal point, central motif or integral part of the overall design and not just added as an afterthought. Varying the type and thickness of thread will alter the final look and, for the best effect, it is preferable to choose a single thread that lies smoothly when you are working stitches that cross over or overlap themselves.

With solid items such as mirrors, it is necessary to find a stitch that will cover corners or work round the object.

- Cushion (Scotch) stitch will enclose the corners of square objects.
- Norwich (waffle), half Rhodes, a laid grid, varying forms of spider webs or overstitched net will successfully trap mirrors, metals or coins in place.
- Diagonal interlaced cross and walneto will work for a spot motif or when a stitch is required to be incorporated on the diagonal.
- Jessica stitch of any dimension is invaluable for confining shisha mirrors, coins, metal shim or a wire mesh. Metal shims (0.05 mm), being thin and fairly flexible, are easy to cut into

Below left

Sample card showing different methods for applying mirror pieces, metal shim or shisha to canvas using (from top left) a simple foundation grid, interlaced cross, walneto, spider's web, net, Jessica, squared herringbone, half Rhodes, cushion, windmill, Norwich and eyelet stitch.

Below right

Sample card showing different items such as money, mirror pieces, shisha and leather applied to canvas with variations of shisha, buttonhole, chain stitch and a Dorset button.

Sample (Jill Carter) showing metal shim attached with buttonholed rings, shisha stitch, shisha stitches incorporating beads, Dorset button, laid grid with chain stitch, close shisha overstitched with beaded Cretan stitch.

any shape. Holes can also be punched in the shim to create a centre, making it possible to apply with stitches such as windmill or diagonal eyelet.

- Coins with centre holes are also quite a novelty. They can be applied with stitches formed in the manner of a clock with the centre holes embellished with beads or French knots.
- Shisha stitch and its variations offer more useful and decorative options.
- Edging the objects with either a backstitch or chain stitch is a discreet way of covering any unsightly sides or thicker mirror edges when proper shisha/mica mirrors are unavailable.
- Basic buttonholed rings or their development, 'Dorset buttons', add another choice for applying circles to the canvas ground.

CREATIVE IDEAS

You can create abstract designs and apply a wonderful miscellany of strange or everyday objects to your canvas, although to be successful they would need to be a considered part of the framework of your design. This will, of course, make the piece of work impractical, as you will not want to sit on straws, shells or stones, but you will have immense fun and take on a good challenge, nevertheless. Your inspiration might well start from the textures you have put onto your canvas in the first instance or merely from the object itself.

Drinking straws

Drinking straws come in lots of different colours, can be cut to size, or shaped and could be couched on in any of the ways already mentioned, but with the use of the relevant different thickness of threads and size of stitches. Being hollow, straws can also be stitched through the centre or enhanced with other items pushed through the tube. They can be arranged in pattern, blocks or used singly (see the embroidery on page 59).

Hand-made paper tubes or wire 'beads'

Hand-made paper tubes or wire beads can also be sewn on by stitching through the centre tube or catching the edges. Various shapes of paper bead can be accomplished by varying the geometric shapes to be cut out and rolled up. If you do not have a gadget for winding paper tubes, roll the paper shape round a cylindrical object such as a pencil or needle. A small dab of glue on the finishing edge will keep the roll in place.

Even without a winding tool, you can still make wire coils or 'beads' by wrapping the wire round a nail, pencil, needle or something similar, adjusting the size to your own requirements. Pushing the wire through tubular ribbon or free machining it before turning it into a coil will enable you to match or contrast your colour scheme and incorporate another interesting texture.

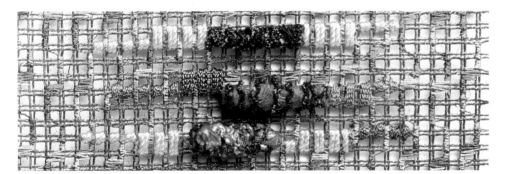

TIPS

- Use decorative paper to make 'beads'.
- Cut the edges of the shape with decorative scissors before rolling the 'bead'.
- Embellish the completed paper tube or 'bead' with metallic or texture paint (see page 111).
- Varnish the completed paper tube or 'bead' with exotic nail varnish.

Right
Painted Tissuetex stitched to the canvas showing sticks, a bamboo brush protector, rippled wire, paper and machine-wrapped wire 'beads', applied with fly, straight and satin stitches. Free, straight stitch machining, tied oblong cross and satin stitches divide the textures.

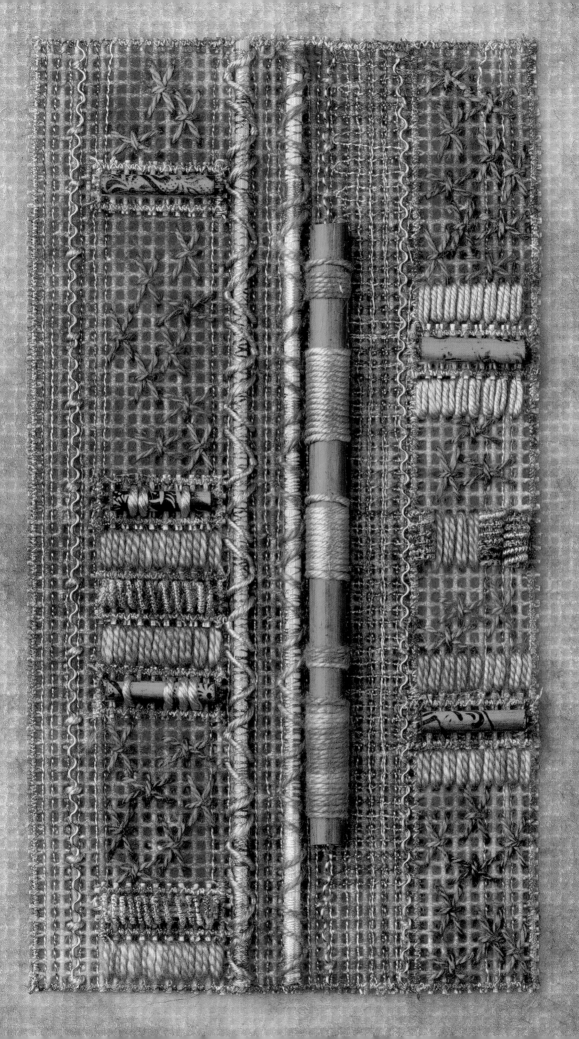

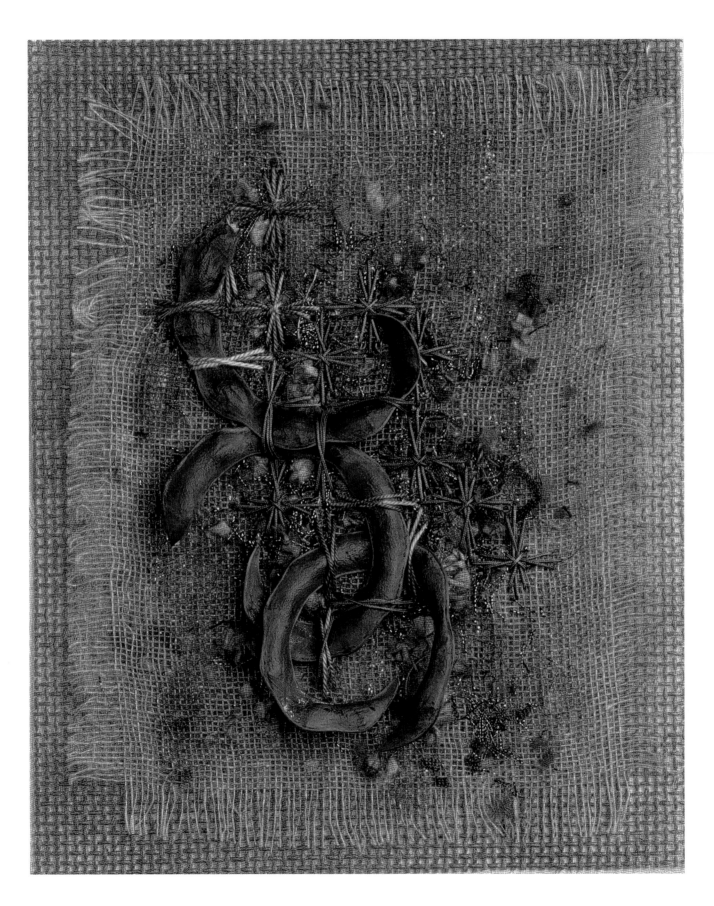

Sticks

Sticks, twigs, seed pods or food shapes (pasta etc.) can all be applied with couching or canvas work stitches and combined with canvas work embroidery as appropriate, adjusting the type of thread for the size of stick. They work well, creating or accentuating line and form. The choice of threads depends on what suits the design and, as these are simple line applications, more exotic or textured canvas work stitches can be chosen for the surrounding areas.

Irregular shapes

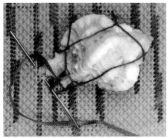

Stones, shells or objects with an irregular shape without holes through which to sew are easily managed with either a laid grid, shisha stitch, buttonhole stitch or needleweaving techniques. If your object is to be a focal point, it is important to consider its texture and finished height when stitching round it, so that the chosen canvas work stitches complement the applied article and do not 'fight' or detract from it (see photograph on page 68).

Buttons

If you would prefer to keep it simple but equally effective, search your button box. You might suddenly find a use for that special one and only antique button, or even a series of buttons.

ATTACHING OBJECTS ONTO CANVAS

Laid grid

Stabilize the item to be attached with a grid of threads. Stitch as many lines in a grid as are needed to secure the object, in either a regular or irregular criss-cross pattern depending on the shape of the object. Decide how much of the item you want to show. You will not want to detract from a beautifully marked stone, rock or shell with heavy stitching or a complex framework (see the photograph on page 68).

Depending on the shape of the object to be applied, it may be preferable to lay down the warp threads and then to wrap the weft threads once round warp threads.

The sides can be 'shadowed', supported or covered up with clusters of French knots, couching, or a line of back or chain stitch, as long as it all appears to be part of the design.

Where the laid grid is an important feature or integral part of the design, once the covering network has been established, the threads may be overstitched with shisha or buttonhole stitch for extra depth and texture, or colour enhancement.

Left
Seed pods applied with windmill stitch onto a background textured with snippets of thread and fabric bonded to butter muslin and canvas, and overlaid with chiffon.

Your background canvas work stitch and texture needs to work in conjunction with the applied object and should be chosen with due consideration for the design.

Shisha stitch

Shisha stitches are excellent for applying almost any shaped object, as they are most often executed on a laid foundation grid, which will keep the item in place. Shisha stitch is an embroidery stitch well known for being used in a variety of ways on Indian embroidery, but it can be comfortably adapted to apply items on the surface of an already stitched canvas background as illustrated in the photograph below.

Whether it is a mirror, metal sheet, button or coin to be applied, the shisha stitches may be worked traditionally or freely on and around a foundation grid with varying lengths of stitch to secure the object in place. Alternatively, as the foundation grid is laid, it can be pulled off centre, so that the final effect will be less structured and more randomly shaped.

Applying larger objects combined with a range of canvas stitches. From the top: Shell skeleton applied with free Cretan stitch on top of reversed Hungarian stitch. Shell applied with buttonhole stitch beside upright cross, brick and t-stitch. Shell applied with shisha stitch beside double straight cross, alternating oblong cross and crossed Gobelin. Shell showing foundation grid and the start of shisha stitch with random tent and satin stitch background. Coral applied with needleweaving beside jacquard and upright oriental.

Choose a canvas work stitch to 'grow' into the applied objects and the decorative shisha stitches and one that does not overpower the effect you have already created. Variations of tent or Alicia's lace or a simple background pattern darning to give just a hint of texture or colour will often suit admirably.

TIP

- It is preferable to use a single twist thread for the stitching, as the appeal, texture and formation of the stitch is 'cleaner' and more easily distinguishable.

Buttonhole stitch

Buttonhole stitch (and its variations taken from the family of needle lace fillings) is another useful basic stitch to enclose and contain an unconventionally shaped object on canvas work.

Initially it may be necessary to stabilize the item with temporary overstitching, tacking or double-sided sticky tape, until enough of the buttonhole stitch has been worked up to hold it in place. Start off (as you would for a basic needle lace filling) with a backstitch outlining the object. Into this foundation line of backstitches, work your buttonhole stitch or a suitable variation of your choice. To echo and follow the shape being applied it may be necessary to increase or decrease the buttonhole stitches. Additional stitches doubled up or placed at intervals into the spaces created by the previous row of buttonholing will lengthen and widen the shape. Working the stitches into alternate spaces will reduce and tighten up the shape (see second shell down, on opposite page).

TIP

- This is another technique that could be adopted for applying items on the surface of an already stitched canvas.

Needleweaving

Needleweaving is a technique generally associated with drawn thread techniques and often used for decorative borders. The threads are withdrawn from the ground and the remaining warp threads are gathered up and needlewoven into straight bars or to form linking patterns.

With thick or thin threads as appropriate to the design, long straight threads can be 'spun' from a central point, or laid close together and then woven with a darning stitch or embellished with buttonhole stitch.

Further straight lines may be extruded from the needleweaving as you work to create different shapes and extensions from the main body. Free and abstract needleweaving over the surface of stitched canvas work is useful for adding texture, creating drama and specific focal points for a two-dimensional look.

Detail showing needleweaving techniques (see also page 7).

7 Drawn–thread techniques on canvas

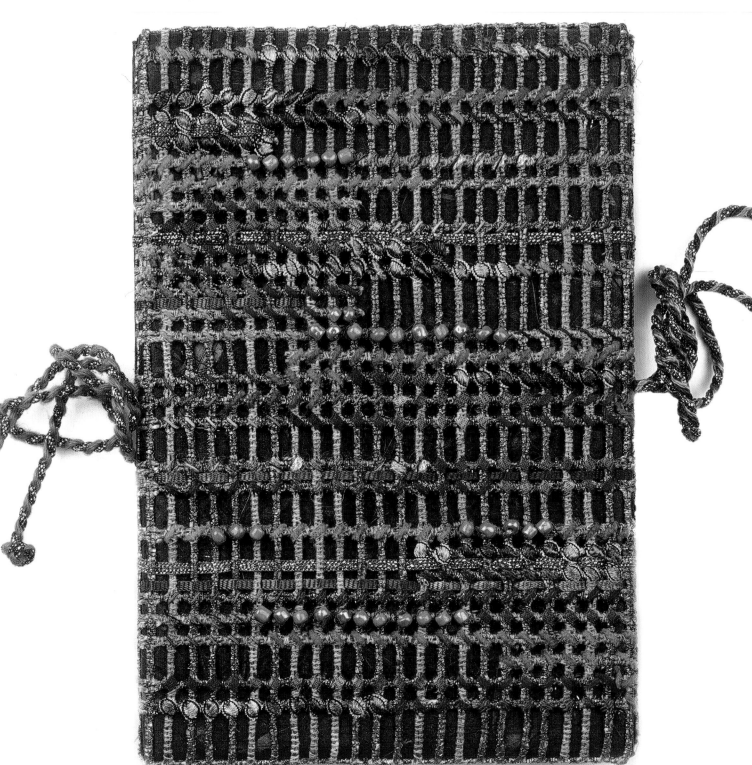

DRAWN THREAD

Drawn-thread embroidery, characterized by its withdrawn areas, open hem-stitched borders and needleweaving designs, was traditionally worked in white or natural colours to display the decorative stitching and emphasize the positive and negative aspects of the technique.

Normally the threads used to work this technique are slightly thinner than the ground fabric, in order that the effect rather than the stitch is the more prominent feature.

The possibilities presented by the withdrawal of threads on larger canvas will broaden the horizons for experimenting and developing non-representational canvas work. It is, of course, a little harder to withdraw the threads as the background has been sized, but with care and patience the threads may be removed in the usual manner.

Drawn-thread techniques, such as needleweaving and Hardanger, readily translate from their usual even-weave fabric background onto a canvas background and offer the same opportunities as if worked on an even-weave fabric.

Combining canvas work stitches, changing the thickness of the stitching threads and the withdrawal of the background canvas threads create all manner of possibilities and potential for developing both techniques to bring a fresh dimension to canvas work.

NEEDLEWEAVING

Withdrawing either the warp or weft threads will leave a grounding of lines on which to work a choice of needleweaving or drawn-thread techniques. Clusters of these remaining threads are either collected up to form bunches, or needlewoven into decorative patterns. Usually these come in the form of attractive bands or borders. The deeper the withdrawn-thread section, the more ornate and complex a decorative pattern can be worked. Needleweaving is generally worked in a figure-of-eight motion with the needle and thread going over and under a chosen number of threads.

Left
Concertina Book Cover (Jill Carter) showing background canvas textured with machine stitching. Canvas threads were withdrawn to create open and solid areas. The solid areas have been over stitched with variations of tent stitch in different textured threads and incorporating woven braids. Hand-twisted cords form the ties.

Right
Beaded four-sided stitch outlines a rectangle of Kloster blocks and cushion stitches for a simple design that could be tessellated. Machine-wrapped bars support a woven filling. Jessica's stitch, beaded tent, arrowhead and cushion stitches repeat in bands either side of the Hardanger outline.

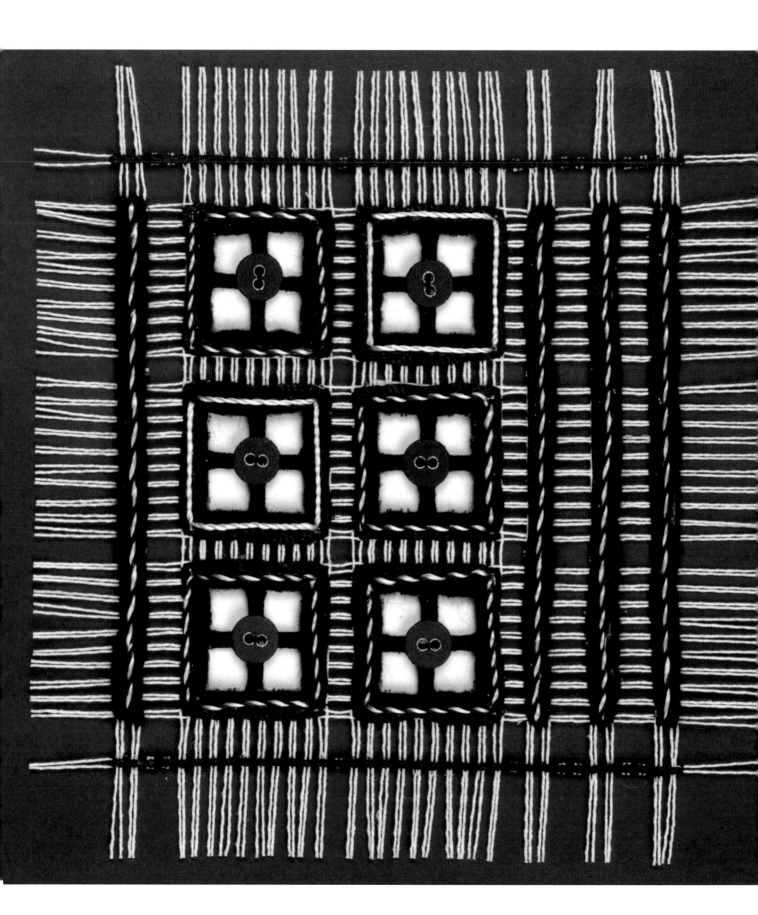

A selection of cotton perles, knitting ribbon and alpaca wool.

HARDANGER EMBROIDERY

The traditional whitework technique of Hardanger (so called after a region in Norway) is recognizable by its characteristic satin stitch outlining Kloster blocks, which form the basis of its familiar geometric designs and the cutting and withdrawal of threads within these areas. The grid of threads left in situ are overstitched with needleweaving and the spaces filled with intricate and lacy fillings.

The essential elements of traditional Hardanger may be successfully transferred onto canvas with an 18- or 22-count or Congress cloth, which comes in a 22- and 24-count. There is the added bonus that Congress cloth comes in many different colours, should you wish to work in colours. Larger count canvas will present opportunities for working Hardanger techniques more freely.

THREADS

Traditional Kloster blocks, which form the geometric patterns, will need to be worked in threads of a suitable thickness relative to the background canvas. Your stitching thread for the Kloster blocks and surface stitches should be slightly thicker than the background thread, and slightly thinner for the pulled thread and filling stitches work.

'Hardanger' with the machine: Straight stitches in ribbon and wool were overstitched with free straight stitch machining to replace the Kloster blocks. The threads were cut away and needlewoven by hand, in the usual manner, with a button centre. Close satin stitch machining and overstitched bands contain the design so that warp and weft threads are secure.

Working on a slightly larger background canvas will give you lots of leeway and freedom to find a different range of threads to use. To enrich the technique with a more dramatic and contemporary approach but keeping to the traditional stitches, expand and use a range of exciting white threads to encompass matt, shiny, textured, iridescent, silk, wool, rayon, braid or cord. Blending filament is a valuable texture to consider incorporating in your embroidery as it is combined with the working thread so that the metallic element of the thread gently glistens and shimmers through the stitches.

Metallic threads will add their own dynamics to any piece of embroidery and Hardanger is no exception. Pulling and weaving with metallics is not as easy as using cotton or silk, but, if you take time with your stitching technique, they will give you the outcome you are looking for and add sparkle. Metallics come as braids, cords or threads and in a wide range of shades of copper, gold and silver, in addition to an amazing collection of colour mixes and combinations.

COLOUR

Altering the thickness of thread and introducing colour will change the essence and look of Hardanger embroidery, but moving into colour is fun and many of the effects will develop into interesting surface stitchery to combine or contrast with canvas work stitches.

Although the sensational assortment of multi-coloured threads are very popular and have crept into Hardanger embroidery, working with them does not always result in the effect you think you are going to achieve. As always, it is a good idea to work a small practice piece to be certain that you like the effect.

Even working in colours, the most successful results for any of the drawn-thread techniques included in Hardanger embroidery, such as reversed diagonal faggoting, are achieved using the same colour thread as the background. Like all drawn-thread stitches this stitch creates and relies on small, tightly pulled holes for impact, and this easily disappears with contrasting or multi-colours.

TIP

- Check that your choice of threads are colour-fast, as it would be devastating if they were to bleed into other colours when the canvas work is dampened and stretched.

CREATIVE IDEAS

Working on canvas will present opportunities for varying the scale of the ground fabric and thereby the threads. Combining canvas work stitches and the withdrawal of the background canvas will create all manner of possibilities for creative development and will add variety and interest to the final design. Experiment with the following:

- Work Hardanger outlines randomly on the background canvas for a different texture or to emphasize and open up specific areas.
- The Kloster blocks may be expanded or irregularly shaped to become a point of interest among traditional canvas stitches, especially large areas of upright ones.
- Work on a larger scale to produce scope for larger, more significant focal points, with Kloster blocks stitched in thicker threads or ribbons.
- Transfer-painted backgrounds with a range of colours offer the chance to abandon traditional geometric shapes to follow lines of colour freely.
- Traditional geometric Hardanger designs can be abandoned and smaller areas of Kloster blocks can be incorporated in the body of a design for accents or spot texture.
- Weave torn sheers or ribbons through needlewoven bars to create bands of texture and interest in an abstract design.
- Encompass various different items at the bar junctions, such as buttons or tied ribbon, for added accents.

Random Hardanger techniques on painted fusible webbing background with dove's eye filling, beaded and unbeaded, eyelets and upright cross (drawn-thread technique). Fringe stitch edges the sample.

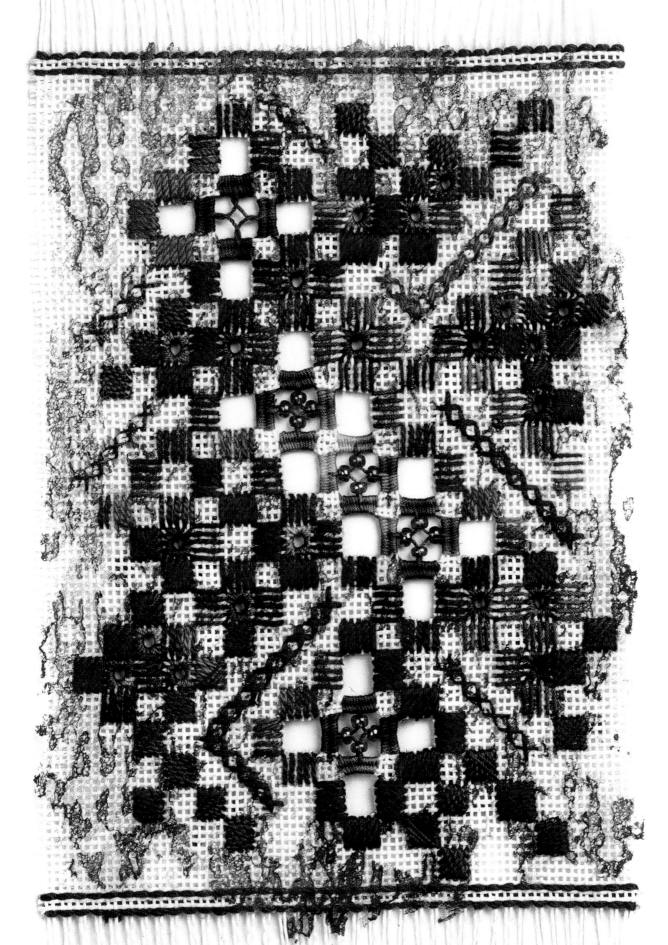

8 Pulled thread on canvas

PULLED THREAD

Traditionally worked on linens of varying thicknesses or on fine muslins, this whitework embroidery technique moves seamlessly onto canvas with its even-weave background.

The negative spaces and patterns created by the pulled threads (also known as drawn fabric) are the focus of the technique, characterized by the gathering up of single or clusters of ground threads, which are then pulled tightly to form the decorative patterns. The small working stitches creating the pattern of holes are supposed to merge into the background fabric, hence traditionally the stitches were usually worked with white or cream threads on a corresponding white or cream background.

The development of pulled-thread patterns varies from being stitched and formed in squares, on the diagonal, and on the straight (up and down or left and right). As a general rule, the thread is pulled away from the hole into which it has just entered in order to form the open space effect. The thread must then progress to the next stage in such a manner that the newly formed hole is not blocked by any trailing threads passing behind. The amount of tension on the working thread governs the size of the hole created in the pattern and the width of the stitch being formed, but it usually looks more professional if pulled tightly.

The pleasure of this traditional technique is found in the simple patterns and clean lines. Overall the technique works best, even on canvas, when the threads match the ground in order to highlight the negative effects, but if you want to branch out into a coloured canvas, Congress cloth, which comes in a range of colours, is a useful choice.

CANVAS

Taking the technique onto a canvas ground calls for some adjustments to the working process. For a start a good quality woven mono canvas (and not an interlocking canvas) is required, where the component threads will move easily when pulled. The pulling tension of a working thread will easily cut through the mesh threads of a cheap canvas, so choose the best quality canvas.

It is important to choose a mesh size relevant to your design and the final effect you wish to achieve, bearing in mind that the background threads of the canvas are a visible factor in the patterns. Work done on a higher count canvas and stitched with equivalent threads will produce delicate and lacy results, whereas lower count canvas will be more appropriate for a contemporary approach with the use of thicker threads to complete the pulled thread stitches.

In certain instances the canvas may be washed to soften it, but this is not always appropriate, and the canvas must be completely dry and pulled back into shape before the embroidery is started.

Pulled Thread Bag (Jill Carter) based on the bar code theme that incorporates a variety of textured threads. Braids are couched with machine stitches and free cable stitch is worked between the gobelin zigzag border pattern. Pulled thread stitches include diagonal cross filling, four-sided stitch, ringed backstitch (beaded) reversed diagonal faggoting (beaded and unbeaded) in conjunction with long-armed cross stitch and diagonal mosaic,
a braid stitch edging and hand-twisted cord handles.

THREADS

For working on canvas, a robust single, smooth-textured thread is needed as it has to hold the tension of the pulled stitches. It is advisable not to have the thread too long as it could break with constant pulling. It is, of course, possible to use threads of more than one strand, such as silks, cottons etc., but the strands have to be lined up carefully and kept flat as the stitch is made.

PULLED-THREAD STITCHES ON CANVAS

With a contemporary interpretation on canvas the rules for pulled-thread techniques are refashioned. The essence of pulled-thread embroidery with regular patterns and negative and positive areas can be exploited with appealing textured surface stitchery and creative effects using paint, thread and stitch. Incorporating embroidery or canvas stitches, adding beads or woven threads will add another dimension.

With the surface-painting techniques, small unpainted areas might appear when the threads are gathered up tightly. These can be masked with water-based coloured pencils or the fabric paint felt-tip pens chosen to match the background colours.

Choose your pulled thread stitches to complement and work in conjunction with the canvas work stitches. Not all the patterns behave on canvas as they would on a fabric and not all the patterns look effective on canvas, so it is worth working small samples to check that you have decided on the one most sympathetic to your design.

TIPS

- A stiletto or awl is an important tool for helping to reposition the canvas threads.
- Use a stiletto to create or enlarge eyelets in stiff canvas where the making of the initial hole in the appropriate place makes it easier to pull the stitch into position.

As with the combinations of other techniques and canvas work, pulled-thread stitches must be considered as a part of the whole design and not just included as an afterthought.

- Straight satin stitches can be formed in lines, as outlines or solid blocks and pulled tightly after each stitch is made.
- Reversed diagonal faggoting, upright diagonal crosses and satin stitches (on the diagonal) all relate well with diagonal canvas stitches to make open or contrasting textured lines.
- Blocks of Smyrna crosses can be pulled to create interesting open grid effects or they can be individually outlined with lines of pulled satin stitches.
- Pulled square or diagonal eyelet stitches adapt very successfully to canvas, especially if the central hole is given a helping hand with a stiletto.
- Four-sided stitch (more often a border or edging stitch) and ringed backstitch are stitches worked on the horizontal. Because of the stiffly sized canvas, pulling the stitch tends to drag the thread at an angle, thereby making the pattern slant instead of keeping it at right angles. In both cases, it is preferable to pull and stitch each stage twice to 'set' the stitch. This may mean that the working thread has to be thinner so that it does not cover the holes. On canvas, punch stitch is a better choice than four-sided stitch for filling an area.

Four-sided stitch

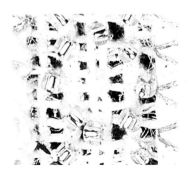

Ringed backstitch

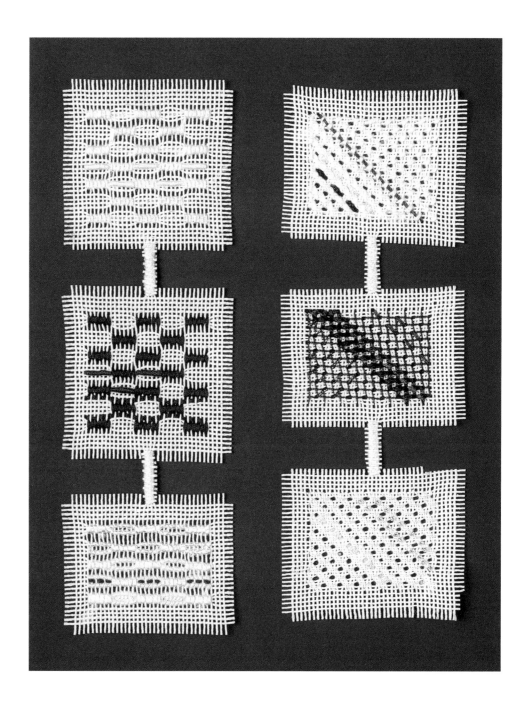

Pulled thread stitches showing (left) satin stitch combinations incorporating bullion knots or woven ribbons (far right) diagonal cross filling with variations of thread, woven ribbon and inclusion of beads.

- Punch stitch is constructed by moving across the area in pairs of stitches over the chosen number of threads, pulling after each stitch. Once the area is filled in one direction the work is turned and the other two sides of the square are stitched in the same manner. By working two sides of the square in sequence and each stitch twice, the stitches and pattern remain neatly perpendicular.

With the wide variety of stitches from which to choose in this technique, it would be worthwhile experimenting with your favourites and creating a portfolio of ideas.

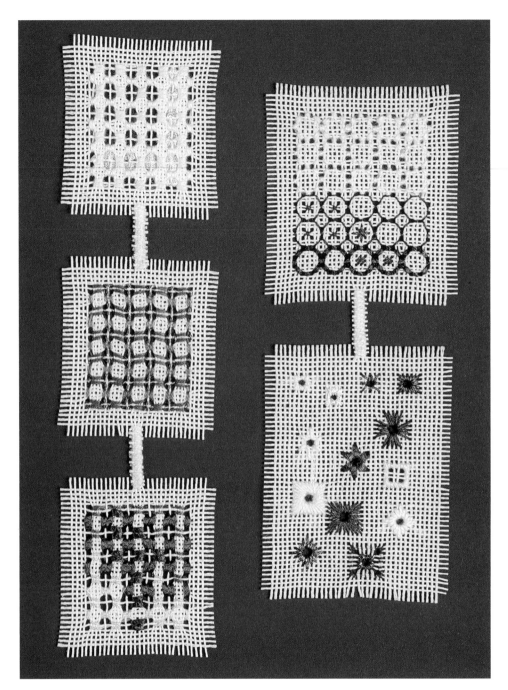

Left
Pulled-thread stitches showing
(left) Framed cross filling with a
range of thread thicknesses and
ribbon weaving; (right) Variations of
ringed back stitch and eyelets in
different thicknesses of thread.

Right
Bag (Jill Carter) combining smyrna
cross stitches and beaded mosaic
stitch with pulled thread techniques
– diagonal eyelet, reversed diagonal
faggoting, diagonal upright cross.

CREATIVE IDEAS

- Choose a larger canvas mesh to accommodate the thicker threads for a much chunkier and more spectacular outcome.
- Finer threads could be used to emphasize the holes created where the stitches are pulled on a large canvas.
- Combine embroidery stitches such as bullion knots for texture.
- Weave ribbons through the holes created by the stitches for a shiny texture against the matt background/threads.
- Use vibrant, shiny knitting ribbons and metallics for a lustrous result.
- Add beads where appropriate for highlighting, shimmer or focus.

9 Machine embroidery on canvas

Machining on canvas will unlock a whole new perspective of stitching and creative development as you exploit the grids or mesh of the canvas. You do not have to be an expert machinist to enjoy machining on canvas, nor do you need the latest in machine technology, although, of course, either of those will further your enjoyment and progress.

Even though machining and machine embroidery techniques are being taken away from their roots of being stitched on a cloth background, it is mostly extremely successful on canvas, introducing and projecting a unique element into creative canvas work. Contrasting surface finishes can be created with zig zag stitching, straight stitch infilling or canvas work stitches being overstitched by machine to flatten and change the levels and depth of texture.

Not all machine embroidery techniques translate onto canvas and some of the effects, which look wonderful on a normal cloth background, may be lost on a canvas ground, so it is worth experimenting on the different types of canvas.

To 'make a statement' or enhance a design, machining on canvas may be approached from two different perspectives – either to decorate the background even-weave mesh or embellish and combine with canvas work stitching. Normal stitching or free machine embroidery techniques can be used depending on the final effects preferred, or a whole design could be worked on a canvas background with the machine, if relevant.

USING THE MACHINE

It is always important to keep your machine in good working order, clear of fluff and oiled (if appropriate) according to the manual, as your machine will be working hard. Before you start serious stitching, don't forget to give your machine a little warm-up with some normal stitching on a spare piece of fabric just to check that everything is operating properly.

Working with a large needle (90/100) is preferable so that, if your machine stitching goes through a canvas thread, the needle will be strong enough to withstand the force. Practise with the threads that you are going to use – the tension can be adjusted if necessary and it will be prepared for stitching the main piece.

Machine embroidery threads have a sheen on them, which will give a marvellous lustre to your stitching and there is a spectacular range of colours, plain or variegated, metallic or iridescent, which will tempt and entice you to stitch. All the usual rules for starting, finishing and tying off your threads apply to machining on a canvas background. Whether you have the same thread top and bottom is a matter of personal choice and experience but, if you are a beginner, it would be more desirable to use the same type of thread on the machine and in the bobbin.

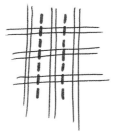

Straight machine stitching between canvas mesh.

Straight machine stitching in both directions between canvas mesh.

It is not necessary to use a hoop (as is usual if working free machine embroidery techniques on fabric) because the canvas is stiff and rigid. However, some canvases do not have a lot of sizing, and it may be necessary to put those into a frame to keep them taut. If you are free machining on a stiff canvas, simply hold the sides of the piece you are stitching and move it where you want it to go as if you were using a hoop. Stitching with a pressure foot on simply requires a guiding hand, just as if you were stitching on a fabric.

STRAIGHT STITCHING WITH A PRESSER FOOT AND THE SETTINGS AT NORMAL

Straight stitching with the 'universal' or 'general' foot is a good place to start if you have limited machining experience. On either a mono or double canvas the spaces between the threads can be straight stitched (with the foot on). Areas can be stitched between the mesh to create a lightly textured filled-in element to your design, which will work well as a contrast to textured canvas work stitches.

CREATIVE IDEAS

- Incorporate fragments of fabric, yarns or other textural items as you straight stitch for a more dimensional outcome.
- Build up wider lines or areas of straight stitching across the canvas so that you can work random areas of hand stitches between the lines.
- On a larger double canvas, weave fabric or ribbon through the open grid and machine through the fabric or ribbon for a raised surface.
- Overstitch straight or diagonal canvas work Gobelin stitches for ridged effects.

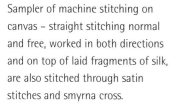

Sampler of machine stitching on canvas – straight stitching normal and free, worked in both directions and on top of laid fragments of silk, are also stitched through satin stitches and smyrna cross.

Close zigzag through satin stitch.

CABLE STITCH WITH THE PRESSER FOOT

This stitch is tremendously effective on canvas to create heavier lines for definition or textural
outlining effects. The technique makes it possible to use a thicker thread that cannot be
threaded through the top of the machine but has to be wound by hand, as evenly as possible,
onto a bobbin. The work is turned over so that the actual machining takes place on the back of
the work, and thick thread textures will appear couched on the underside of what is, in fact, the
front of the work.

Cable stitch can be worked with the 'universal' foot on, using straight stitch, with the resulting
effects dependent on the type of thread that has been wound on the bobbin. It is better not to
try to wrap very hairy threads round the bobbin as the ends tend to get caught up in the
machine and can cause problems. The design may be drawn on the back of the work so that
you can follow the lines with your straight stitching, and it is important to consider carefully what
colour will be showing up on the front. The lower tension will generally have to be loosened to a
greater or lesser degree to accommodate the heavier thread – it is worth experimenting, in
addition to adjusting the stitch length, until you find the effect you are after.

Cable stitch with the presser foot.

ZIGZAG/SATIN STITCHING WITH A PRESSER FOOT AND THE SETTINGS AT NORMAL

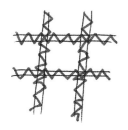

Open zigzag over canvas grid.

If you have a swing needle sewing machine, you will be able to achieve open zigzag, satin stitch and decorative effects. For perfect satin stitch, check and adjust the stitch tension before you start, to ensure that the top thread locks with the bobbin thread on the underside of the stitching, so that no bobbin thread is visible on the surface. (If you turn the canvas over, you should be able to see the threads locking underneath on the edge.) This will give you a smooth top surface, which is important if working a close satin stitch, unless you have a particular requirement for a rough texture with the threads locking on the top or at the sides. With the width set at the required span, the length needs to be adjusted to make closely packed stitches to the density you require. Depending on the thickness, if you are going to stitch on top of wool canvas work stitches, it may be necessary to change your standard presser foot to the embroidery foot, which has a small gully underneath running up the middle to accommodate bulk and allow the stitching to move more freely under the foot without piling up.

Machining on a rug canvas and with an open zigzag over the grid will alter the surface texture of the canvas. Light and open canvas work stitches can be overlayered on the top. Changing the top and bobbin thread to stitch with variegated or different coloured threads will further vary the outcome, with the bobbin colour just peeping through the top thread colour on the sides if you adjust the tension accordingly. Before starting, work a few practice pieces to fit the zigzag stitch to the count of the canvas ground you have chosen.

Using a close machine satin stitch will cover and gather together the threads of a double canvas, thereby enlarging the spaces between the stitched grid, which could be built up with a selection of different textured threads woven through the mesh and then further overstitched.

Raised lines for surface texture can be formed by machine couching a thicker decorative thread or cord with satin stitching. This is a useful means of accentuating or shadowing canvas line stitches or creating more dominant grid lines, such as a diagonal trellis effect, to enclose canvas work stitches. A braiding foot, where the thread is passed through the small hole in the front of the foot ready for overstitching, is very useful for helping to keep the couched thread straight and in position as it is machined but, if you do not have this attachment, simply hold in place the thread for couching and zigzag over it.

CREATIVE IDEAS

- Alter the zigzag stitch from narrow to wide to create interesting lines of varying dimensions on the canvas surface, which will pick up and enclose either one or two threads.
- Stitch across the canvas to form interesting areas to offset and enclose canvas work stitches.
- Stitch random lines of machining to add texture to an open background.
- Try cable stitch with a narrow zigzag stitch.

If your machine has a tailor tacking foot (generally used as the basting foot in dressmaking), you will have enormous fun creating appealing loop effects, which would easily substitute for velvet stitch or Ghiordes knot in canvas work embroidery. Varying the width and length will

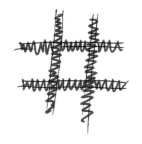

Close zigzag over canvas grid.

Right
Changing the surface texture of a double canvas with close zigzag, incorporating woven torn strips of fabric and top stitched with triple zigzag.

Left
Grid (Pam Watts) with machine-wrapped grid over a textured background fabric and overstitched with raised chain band using a fine machine-wrapped cord.

considerably alter the outcome, and it is important to experiment until you find the effect you need. For representational embroidery you will be able to machine across the canvas, creating depth and texture where it is required, and the whole process is a lot speedier than some of the three-dimensional canvas work stitches. As the stitch is simply a basting stitch, which pulls out very easily, it needs securing – either overstitched with an open zigzag, or lightly dabbed with PVA on the underside of the canvas to solve the problem.

CREATIVE IDEAS

- Stitch lines close together for a packed-in three-dimensional effect.
- Cut the loops to create a fringe.

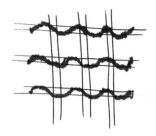

Automatic pattern worked in the centre of double mesh.

AUTOMATIC PATTERNS WITH A PRESSER FOOT AND THE SETTINGS AT NORMAL

The decorative patterns found on most modern sewing machines will give you a wealth of choices for experimenting with pattern on a canvas background. The more definite patterns are particularly effective for altering the canvas surface if they are worked down the centre of a double canvas. It is worth trying out the different patterns that you have available on your own machine with different count double canvas to see what gives you the most interesting results.

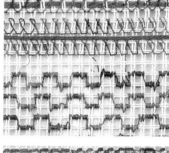

CREATIVE IDEAS

- Experiment with some of the ideas mentioned above, but substitute a decorative pattern for the straight or satin stitch.
- Overstitch canvas or embroidery stitches with a decorative stitch to flatten the textures and create another dimension to the background.
- Join different count canvases together with a decorative stitch to make a feature of the line.
- Try cable stitch with a decorative automatic pattern.

FREE STITCHING WITH THE MACHINE

Even more compelling opportunities are revealed with free machining on canvas. Using the darning foot and lowering the feed dog/teeth (or covering the plate) will enable you to move the canvas freely in any direction to create your own design on the background or to overstitch canvas work stitches to make interesting surface variations. Darning feet come in a variety of sizes and shapes and, although there are instances when the machine is used without a foot, it is generally safer to stitch with your darning foot in place. Your sewing machine manual will help you prepare the machine for free stitching if you are uncertain. To begin stitching, bring the bobbin thread to the surface as you would for free machining on fabric and remember to lower the presser foot lever.

Decorative patterns (with the foot on), including tailor tacking and free zigzag cable stitch.

Free straight stitching

Cuff with reversed cushion stitch separated by straight stitches, free straight stitch machining and tucks with backstitch beaded edging.

Free straight machining between canvas mesh.

The stitching you did with the presser foot on can also be worked freely and you will be able to develop the principles to a far greater extent. Not only will you be able to build up and accentuate your straight machine lines, but you will also be able to meander across the canvas, canvas stitches and open spaces. Free stitching between lines of formed canvas work stitches or patterns significantly changes the look of the surface patterns. With the width and length set at '0', as you are in control of the length and direction of the stitching, it is important to move the canvas smoothly underneath the darning foot, in unison with the speed of the sewing machine, which necessitates being run fairly fast.

The most powerful aspect of free straight stitching is the interaction with canvas work stitches, particularly cushion (Scotch) stitch. This wonderfully versatile stitch, which can be worked with very many variations, lends itself to being overstitched with machining. The balance of the canvas and thread can be varied appreciably with surprisingly different results. Winning combinations of machine and hand stitching work together to develop into either an area of a design or an interesting abstract background pattern.

CREATIVE IDEAS

- Use chunky wools to form the canvas work stitches. Flatten and overlay the corners with straight stitching to form a textured pattern.

Granite stitch

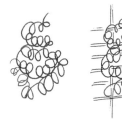

See the photograph of 'Shell Structure' on page 52.

Granite stitch is a useful and constructive development of free straight stitch where the stitch may be used to fill an area. When you move the canvas with a circular motion, overlapping circles can be created on the canvas ground. This technique can be employed to fill in or flatten the canvas background or to work between other textures and canvas work stitches.

Granite stitch (left) and granite stitch on canvas.

CREATIVE IDEAS

- Weave torn strips of fabric through a large canvas mesh. Work granite stitch on top to create a textured background fabric, which would be suitable for a three-dimensional project
- Develop the idea and cut up the machined piece to apply to another background canvas.

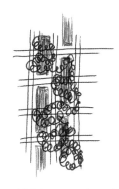

Free cable stitch

You will be able to develop cable stitch further by working it freely with straight stitching to intensify the accumulation of texture and cause it to spill out along the line of stitching. Unique effects can be created with a heavier hand embroidery or textured knitting thread wound onto the bobbin. Keep the stitch length and width at '0' and the lower tension loosened to accommodate the chosen thickness of the thread before experimenting on a sample to discover what effects you can achieve simply by the way you move the canvas – back and forth or gently manoeuvring it to and fro sideways in a circular motion – to create more dense textural effects or even a figure of eight movement.

Strips of fabric woven through the canvas grid and overstitched with granite stitch.

Free straight cable stitch.

CREATIVE IDEAS

- Try cable stitch on a free zigzag setting (which is only just swinging from side to side) and vary the way in which you move the canvas to build up the line against flatter canvas stitches.
- Develop the texture by overlapping your stitches or machining lines very close together.

Free cable stitch in figure-of-eight movement.

Cable stitch border (see photograph on page 77).

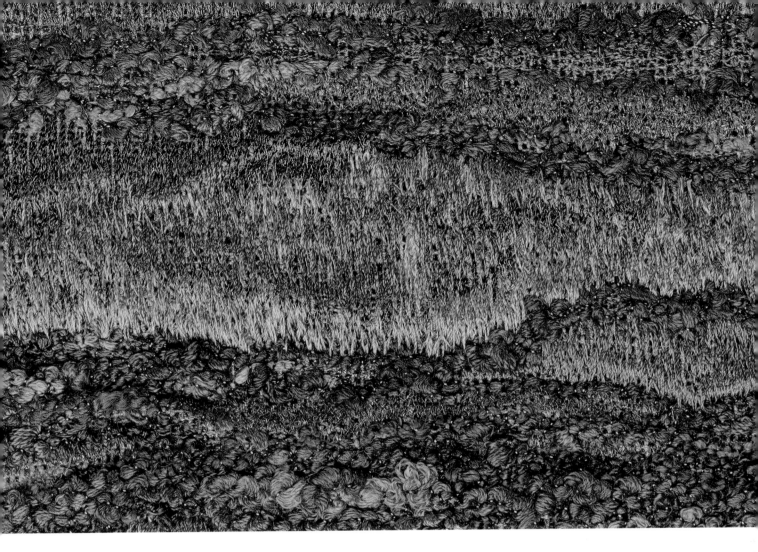

Above

Strata (Pam Watts) using cable stitch, and free machine zigzag on canvas. The canvas was manipulated while damp to form a raised surface.

Left

Free machine cable stitch on an old leaf petiole of a Silver-backed Palmetto from Windermere Island, Bahamas. Strips or sections could be cut up or pulled apart and further applied on to canvas for texture.

Free zigzag stitch worked sideways over canvas.

Free zigzag stitch

Decorative zigzag stitch worked freely will cover areas of the canvas ground for texture. With the machine set up for free machining and the stitch width on zigzag, as wide as you like, you will be able to achieve a variety of effects depending on how you move the canvas and how fast the machine is being run. It is always worth taking some time out to practise the effect you are looking for before starting. Machining straight down, but slightly moving the canvas from side to side will give a jagged look. Moving the canvas fast will open up the zigzag effects and moving it slowly will give you a more close-set formation. Moving round in a circular movement will emphasize a spiral and you will be able to create curves or textured lines by swinging from side to side with a larger sweep for landscape or watery effects. Canvas stitches can also be worked and then overstitched with the machine for further texture and colouring.

As with normal satin stitch, free satin stitch is an effective way of couching down a textured thread or cord for a less structured end result. Machine-wrapped cords can also be made and couched to the canvas ground, perhaps with a more open satin stitch, or with an invisible thread – whichever is the more appropriate for the design.

CREATIVE IDEAS

- Adjust the tension, width of stitch and colour combinations for different results.
- Join different count canvas together to form a background of different dimensions on which to stitch or machine.

Beads sewn on with free zigzag

Beads pre-threaded onto a string are quickly applied with free stitching to give a raised shiny surface. Adjust the width of the stitch to a narrow zigzag or to suit your project and lower the top tension slightly. If you do not want your thread to show, use an invisible top thread. Push the beads into position as you machine, using the end of a barbecue or cocktail stick, and zigzag slowly between each bead to couch down the threading string.

Drawn thread stitching on canvas

The nature of a single weave canvas lends itself to having either the warp or weft threads withdrawn and the remaining ones being overstitched with a free zigzag or satin stitch. Working with a wide zigzag and stitch length at '0' enables you to gather up a collection of canvas threads as you machine. Background effects for trees or landscape suddenly emerge, especially if the count is quite small. This can be done methodically or at random, moving across the withdrawn area to create interesting lines and form.

If bands of vertical or horizontal threads are withdrawn in a more structured way, it will be possible to mirror hand techniques, incorporate a variety of different textured threads or fabric by weaving through the remaining grid, either for overstitching or simply for a different, but decorative look. Narrower bands of withdrawn threads could include and imitate random needleweaving patterns.

Additionally, a wide satin stitch to emulate Kloster blocks from Hardanger embroidery techniques will open the door either to structured or random cutting and withdrawing of threads, to leave a grid for further overstitching, weaving or embellishing.

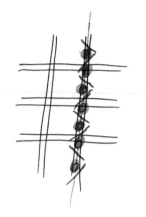

Beads applied with a zigzag stitch.

Below
Machined drawn thread sample on double canvas textured with open zigzag stitching. Withdrawn warp threads leave weft threads to be clustered for a decorative border with free zigzag stitching or woven with ribbon or braid. Tucks were formed with straight stitching or overstitched with zigzag.

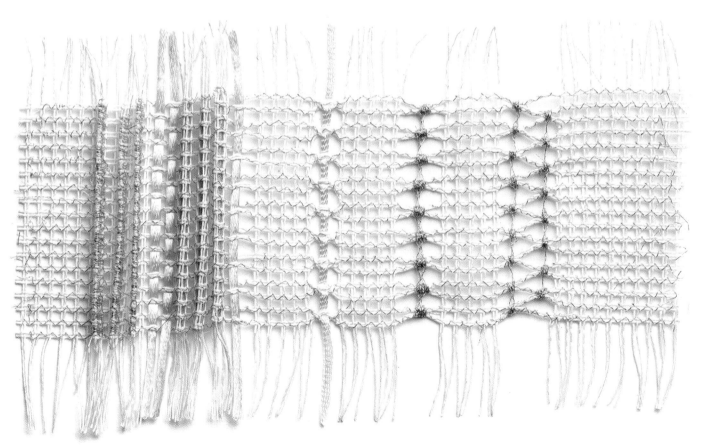

Hungarian Boxes (Jill Carter) shows a range of novelty yarns, wools, silk and ribbons used for Hungarian stitch variation form the textured repeating pattern. Whipped chain and double knot stitch added extra height and texture. The hand stitching is covered with free straight stitch machining incorporating strings of beads applied by free zigzag machining. Norwich (waffle) stitch on paper and canvas forms the 3-D tassel heading and spot motif to echo the Hungarian stitch diamond pattern with French knots for the centre spaces.

Eyelets

Holes or eyelets can be produced by machine in a variety of ways on the canvas. If your machine has an eyelet plate you will be able to follow the instructions in your manual to make the eyelets. Similarly, if your machine has the ability to stitch buttonholes there may well be a circular one that could be adapted and stitched onto canvas. Otherwise there are accessories available (such as one called a Flower Attachment) which will shape and form circles of varying sizes and densities. It may be necessary to trim away whiskers of the ground threads from the middle once the eyelet has been stitched. Combined with other hand techniques, machine-made eyelets add useful contrasting shape and form against straight geometric lines or grids.

If structured eyelets are not for you, try punching a hole in the canvas and working free straight stitch round the open hole. Make your first straight guiding lines at 12, 3, 6 and 9 o'clock and then work round the circle building up the straight stitches. These can be of any length to suit the project or to give a haphazard, uneven definition. Different effects are achieved depending on which type of canvas you are using as a ground fabric. If the sizing on the canvas is minimal, the stitching will probably drag the ground fabric back and enlarge the hole, and irregular shapes can be formed, if necessary, for the design.

Three-dimensional and water-soluble effects

Machining on net can create surface texture to be applied to canvas for a three-dimensional effect. A mixture and diversity can be achieved with layering of nets or transparent fabrics stitched with textured machine embroidery and then applied to the canvas ground, with possibilities presenting themselves for cutting away areas to expose stitching on the canvas or colour contrasting underneath the layers.

Machining on water-soluble 'fabrics' will bring a whole new facet to the contemporary aspect of canvas work embroidery. The free stitching of lacy effects and layering will generate depth and provide scope for enhancing and embellishing canvas work stitching.

The possibilities for creating and applying three-dimensional shapes, flowers, leaves and textures are numerous. There are many books that cover and describe the techniques for machining on water-soluble fabrics, which are worth referring to if you want to develop this aspect of your machining skills.

CREATIVE IDEAS

* Trap other items such as ribbons, beads or small pieces of fabric or thread between the layers of water-soluble fabric for additional effects and colour contrasts.

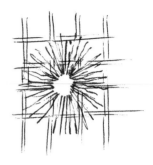

Free straight stitching worked round an open hole or cut to form a decorative eyelet.

Right
Using the flower attachment for single and double machined eyelets on canvas, with couched threads and beads on a transfer-painted background and random wheat sheaf stitch. The finished canvas was applied to textured paper.

10 Beads and stitches on canvas

Embellish and add shimmer with beads. Beads bring a vitality and spirit to canvas work embroidery, whether they are used for highlighting, accentuating, as a focal point, or as contrast for areas of smooth or matt stitching.

Today, beads are readily available in a plethora of colours, textures and sizes – matt and shiny, small and large, round and square, long and short, plain and iridescent, clear or lined, plastic, glass, china or polymer clay. The choice is prodigious and it will not be hard to find what you want to suit your design and colour scheme. Moving onto a larger canvas will present different dimensions and a whole new range of choices for bead, thread and stitch.

BEADS ON CANVAS

Basic stitching method

As with most other embroidery techniques, any type of bead can be added and attached to a canvas work design, although it is always preferable to have preplanned the positioning as part of the design and not to add the beads as an afterthought. The usual methods used for applying beads onto fabric will cross over and adapt onto canvas.

Considered or randomly placed beads can be sewn in place simply by bringing the needle and thread to the surface, taking the needle through the bead and then back down either over a mesh thread or to sit in the space between the mesh threads. The size of bead has to be considered with regard to the size of canvas being used. Too small and the bead may disappear through the holes, over-large and they may sit too proud on top of the space or grid. Beads can be applied singly or two or three at a time, depending on the effect required. Use the same method to lay bugle beads.

Right
An interpretation of the design from the datura sketch on page 38, showing an outline of free zigzag machining, incorporating paper and containing simple laid fillings (machine and hand) and beaded mosaic stitch variations.

Left
Mirror shapes, 4 mm cubes (matt and shiny), triangles, bugles and seed beads of varying sizes that can be used with canvas stitches or applied to canvas.

Beads with buttonhole stitch

Seed or bugle beads may be stitched to stand upright in a line to create a ridge, using a variation of buttonhole stitch. Depending on the effect being created, it may be necessary to start off with two beads on the surfacing thread. In this case, the following stitch is taken through the canvas mesh (beside the surfacing thread) and returned back up by way of the top bead in order to stabilize it and form the buttonhole stitch. Place another bead onto the needle and repeat the process by stitching back into the canvas mesh, and so on until the line is completed. An extra bead can be added each time if a spaced line is called for. This means that the first bead on the needle will be left as a 'bridge' and the thread returned back up through the end bead as before. More complex stitching and applying of beads is covered in Chapter 4.

Beads with canvas work stitches

Beads are particularly suited to being incorporated with canvas work stitches and offer you irresistible possibilities for creating shimmering effects, lustrous lines and textures, and highlighting and accentuating specific areas.

It is important that the beads are sewn on with the working thread and added once you have brought the thread to the surface in order that they become an integral part of the stitch pattern. Work any of the stitches in the sequence usual for the stitch, simply adding the bead where appropriate. Keep a good tension as you stitch since this ensures that the bead is contained at the correct angle and that it will not wobble about. Make sure that you choose a bead of the right dimension for the stitch you are working. You will find that the size of bead, needle and thread are germane to a successful outcome and the desired finished effect. There are no strict rules, but obviously a small bead on a large stitch will get 'lost', and vice versa – a large bead on a small stitch could look ungainly or overpowering. It is advisable to work small samples of your ideas before you start, as undoing areas of beaded stitching is very irksome.

Tent stitch

Beads on canvas are familiarly associated with the antique beaded pieces of the Victorian era sewn on with either half cross or tent stitch, typically worked in floral arrangements and filling either parts or all of the design.

Depending on the effect required, it is generally preferable to work on a double canvas, so that the bead sits neatly into the intersection of four threads, in which case the size of bead chosen needs to fit snugly and not drop through. In addition to round seed beads, a tri-cut bead will sit well in the intersections. Delica beads turn out well with an even effect on a 14 (double threads to the inch)-count canvas. If a single canvas is used, the bead will sit on top of the intersection.

Above
Detail from *A Tissue of Contours* (page 27) showing beads applied with buttonhole stitch.

Right
Sampler of stitches incorporating beads as part of the working process. From the top: Parisian, Brick, Hungarian variations; Mosaic, cushion, cushion variations; Diagonal mosaic, milanese, jacquard; Tied oblong cross, rice stitch, reversed diagonal faggoting, four-sided stitch, ringed back stitch; Kloster blocks – dove's eye filling, square filet filling.

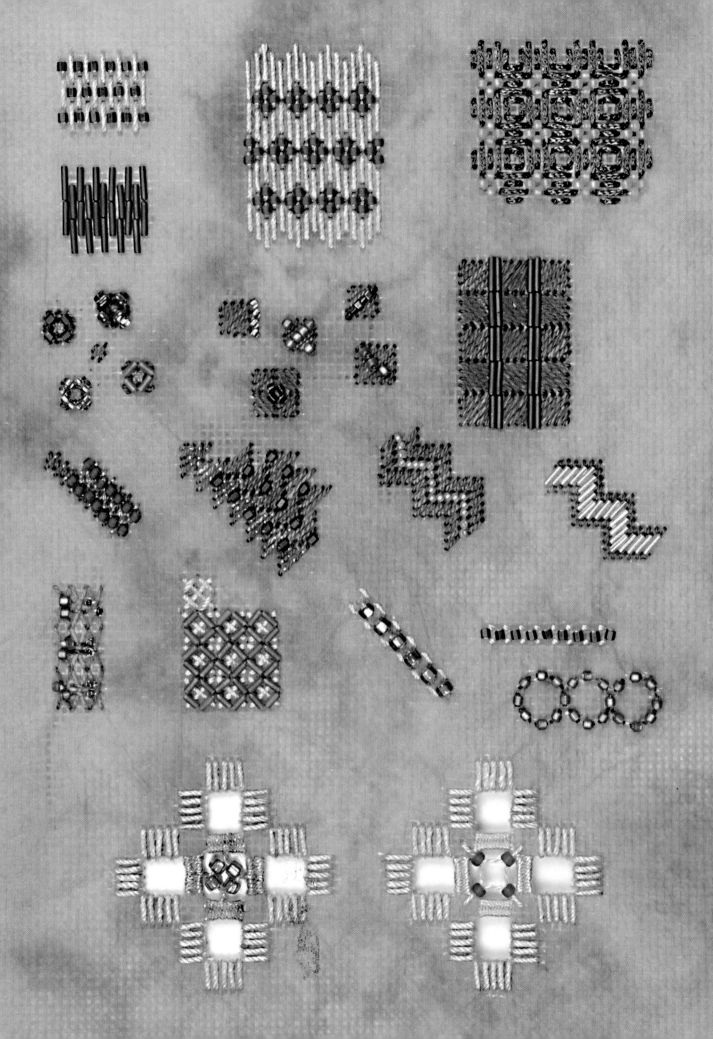

Above

Scissor case (Ann Mockford) showing beaded tent stitch combined with metal thread and Bokhara couching.

Left

Hades II (Ann Mockford) showing a couched metal thread technique combined with beaded tent stitch incorporating tri-cut beads and free-form 'flames' in brick and peyote stitch with a twisted bugle bead fringe.

Work the tent stitch in your chosen method (either continental, half cross or basketweave) and one that is suitable for your design, adding a bead to your thread as you make each individual stitch. There are two principal ways of keeping the bead rigid (see below). Use as strong a thread as possible to stitch on the bead.

1. After working a row of tent stitches, return to the beginning of the next line (and for all subsequent lines of stitching) through the back of your newly formed stitches, taking a backstitch every so often to secure the threads and line of stitchery. This will also tighten up the tension of the stitches so that the beads are held firmly in position at the correct angle on the front.
2. With a double thread, work the tent stitch in either the continental stitch or half cross stitch (or basketweave) method. Make your line of tent stitches as appropriate. To ensure the bead stays in place without twisting or wobbling, return back along the line of your stitching, crossing back over the surface in the opposite direction over each individual beaded tent stitch. As you form the stitch, separate your thread so that it goes either side of the bead and traps it firmly into position.

TIPS

- Another method for stitching on the beads and for added strength and security is to go through each bead a second time.
- Beads and tent stitch can be alternated if the beading is looking crowded.
- Experiment with beads of different types and sizes for an unusual overall texture.

Straight stitches

Straight stitches such as brick, Parisian, Hungarian, etc., offer a profusion of combinations to use with bugle or seed beads. As bugle beads are available in a variety of lengths they may be interchanged with other beads as appropriate to the design, stitch and effect required.

CREATIVE IDEAS

Increase your skills and incorporate beads on your favourite stitches:
- Add beads to the shorter straight stitches for height.
- Add beads in a planned sequence to create patterns or bands of textured stitches.
- Randomly place beads for accent and lift.
- Alternate with yarn stitches as a contrast of textures.
- Use for couching down ribbon or strips of paper.

Cross stitches

It is not always easy to decide where to include beads on cross stitches since the last stitch will always be facing in one direction over the first stitch. In this instance, where the stitch is to contain a bead, you must decide how many beads are required on the stitch – if you only use one bead (depending on the size of both the canvas and bead), it might move up and down the thread like an abacus. This may not be the effect you are trying to achieve. Alternatively, there are opportunities for beaded stitching between or surrounding crosses, which is probably more effective and worthwhile.

Diagonal stitches

Among others, stitches such as mosaic, oriental, Milanese and jacquard move diagonally across the canvas, presenting choices for including bugle or seed beads in diagonal lines, especially useful if your design includes areas where there are diagonals.

CREATIVE IDEAS

- Add beads (one or more) to any of the diagonal stitches forming the block.
- Leave the diagonal stitches unbeaded, but instead separate the lines with one or more lines of beaded diagonal tent stitch (basket weave).

Tied stitches

Certain tied stitches as seen in the family of oblong crosses or wheat lend themselves to being embellished with a final beaded tying stitch.

CREATIVE IDEAS

- Use a beaded tent or straight stitch to tie down the intersections of laid thread fillings.
- Cross the corners of stitches such as rice with a bead.

Straight stitches

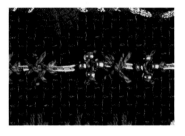

Cross stitches

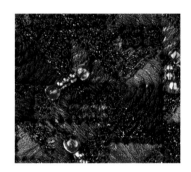

Cushion stitches

Book Cover (Jill Carter) in tapestry wool and novelty yarns with reversed cushion stitches of different dimensions (as seen on the spine) incorporating a large bead and tassel on the centre stitch before free straight stitch machining is worked across the corners. Binding stitch finishes the edges and folded canvas tassels with a machined free cable stitch heading are attached to a hand-twisted cord.

Box stitches

Box stitches (formed by diagonal stitches) such as mosaic or cushion (also known as Scotch) stitch and their many variations open up yet more combinations and possibilities, especially as they can be overstitched to great effect. Sometimes these patterns will comprise tent stitch blocks or outlines.

BEADS WITH PULLED-THREAD TECHNIQUES ON CANVAS

Beads can be used with pulled-thread techniques on canvas as and where appropriate to your design. There is a wide choice of patterns in pulled thread techniques and choosing beads to integrate with the stitches will be determined by the size of the background canvas, the thickness of thread and the effect you want to create.

If you want to combine canvas work stitches with pulled thread techniques and beads on canvas, it is generally preferable to work any of the normal canvas stitches first. Once the canvas threads are pulled and the beads in position, it can be difficult to see where to put the needle into the canvas for the canvas stitches.

As already mentioned, the development of pulled thread patterns varies from being stitched and formed in squares, on the diagonal and on the straight (up and down or left and right), which means that including beads with the working procedures has to be planned according to the way the stitch is structured. Whether you use iridescent or matt beads is a matter of personal choice and dependent on the desired overall effect. The working method follows the usual progress as for pulling thread on an even-weave fabric background, but will require more pulling for the right effect on canvas and to incorporate the beads.

Reversed diagonal faggoting is a particularly effective stitch to bead. Place the bead on the thread when taking the central diagonal stitch. This can be done on each or alternating diagonals. When the working thread returns up the opposite side to complete the second stage of the stitch, it will have to go through the centre bead again to stabilise it. The resulting effect is a textured decorative line to accentuate your design. The beaded diagonal lines may be worked in zigzag or formed into diamond shapes in the same way that the stitch is used without beads.

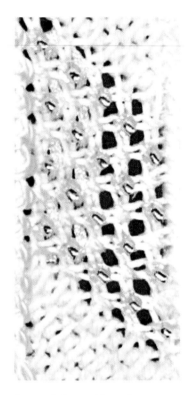

Reversed diagonal faggoting

Beads can be incorporated with stitches worked on the horizontal, such as four-sided and ringed backstitch. Do not forget that on canvas it is preferable to work each stitch twice to 'set' the stitch. The beads can be added to the thread as the stitch is formed on the first journey and the working thread is then taken through the bead again on the second journey. The dimension of the bead is important as each needs room to sit comfortably on the thread in the stitch.

Hems and edges can be further embellished by incorporating beads as the hem stitch is formed. A bead can be effectively substituted for a picot to give an appealing shimmering effect on the edge of your project.

Upright satin stitches are often worked in blocks or square outlines and including beads on the stitches makes interesting outlines or blocks of pattern.

Not all the pulled thread stitches lend themselves to incorporating beads, wholly or partly. It is important that beads should be a considered part of the stitch and it is preferable for them to be static and without the 'abacus effect'. It also defeats the object when the inclusion of beads causes the rhythm of the pulled thread pattern to be lost. You have to be discerning and only use beads in the stitches appropriate to your design and the stitches or pattern that you are working.

BEADS WITH HARDANGER EMBROIDERY TECHNIQUES ON CANVAS

Fillings

Many of the wonderful variety of decorative fillings found in Hardanger embroidery work well with beads. The traditional fillings for Hardanger embroidery will, of course, stand on their own, but introducing beads opens up all sorts of possibilities for enhancing or emphasising the lacy effects. It is important that the beads are considered an integral and connected part of the fillings and not added on afterwards.

Working the filling stitches follows the normal progression, with the beads being added as the filling is formed. The effects differ according to where and when the beads are fed onto the thread and the type of filling being undertaken.

Dove's eye filling is probably one of the most well known of all the Hardanger filling stitches. The different methods of incorporating beads in this filling result in diverse and individual effects, with the beads either coming to the point or on the loops or bars forming the filling. Beads included with the variations of dove's eye fillings also work successfully.

The inclusion of beads in the square filet filling, which echoes the squares of the main needlewoven grid, gives the impression of small knots softening the corners.

Beads can be substituted for French knots on any bar. They can also be incorporated on some of the twisted bars. Here the emphasis will be on the centre of the square since the thread often starts the filling from the centre point.

Not all the fillings look good with beads and, where final result is dependent on perfect, even tension, such as in Greek or spider's web, it is hard to justify adding beads for the sake of it.

The type of bead you use considerably changes the final appearance. Delicate matt beads in the centre of a filling against the same colour ground serve to enhance. Larger ones with a sheen emphasise and create texture as well as lustre. The choice is yours. (For further information refer to my book on Hardanger Embroidery.)

CREATIVE IDEAS

- Have fun exploiting the traditional methods with a change of dimension in canvas.
- Use chunkier threads and beads not normally appropriate to the technique.
- Experiment with canvas work stitches and beaded stitches to capitalise on the variations of thread, texture and dimension.

11 Background stitching for canvas work

There is such an amazing variety of choice available to canvas workers when it comes to deciding on a stitch for a background effect. We are truly spoilt for choices of texture, stitch, line, pattern and effect but, as our selections are so thoroughly personal and subjective, it is worth experimenting with as many variations as possible and not always to play safe with a background that you know will work.

Accommodating elements of your design, whether for traditional or contemporary canvas work, should be carefully calculated to show off the final piece to its best advantage. It is always important to consider your background at the planning stage of your project, to reconcile and consider it as part of the whole and not as an afterthought. Choosing a background for your canvas work is dependent on a whole range of factors in the design and is governed by the type of project you are undertaking – a practical or upholstered piece will need a properly covered ground for longevity, whereas a light and open background of decorative stitching could meet the needs of a panel or hanging that will see no wear and tear.

The balance of the background stitch against the main design is crucial. If you have a delicate central design, device or pattern, it is important not to overshadow it with a heavy background stitch. If your design is rather heavy and solid, a light and airy background pattern may well look insignificant. Where your design is very complex or ornate it will probably require a calm unfussy background to complement it. In short, make sure your background stitch enhances your design. Sometimes, however, there is no specific background stitch to consider as the whole design is the background

As the essence of your finished project can so easily be spoilt by the wrong choices, right at the start, assemble your thoughts methodically to determine what effect you want to achieve and ask yourself some simple questions to determine your objectives:

- Will there be a border as part of the background?
- Is the background to be solid or to have an open texture or pattern?
- Are you going to create a specific effect, e.g. water?
- Do you want a textural background with a mix and range of different stitches?
- Would it suit to have a random open effect with unstitched areas?
- Should gold threads be incorporated?
- Finally, is what you have decided upon practical or suitable for the proposed project and does it add to the whole and show off your finished piece to the best advantage?

TIP

- Shaded threads will change the look of stitch and pattern with their colour variations.

Above
Background stitch detail from *Pineapple* on page 49.

Right
Background stitch 'hanging' presented so that additional samples may be added and showing (left) pattern darning, jacquard, laid pattern; (right) framed cross filling, reversed cushion and brick (Gobelin) stitch.

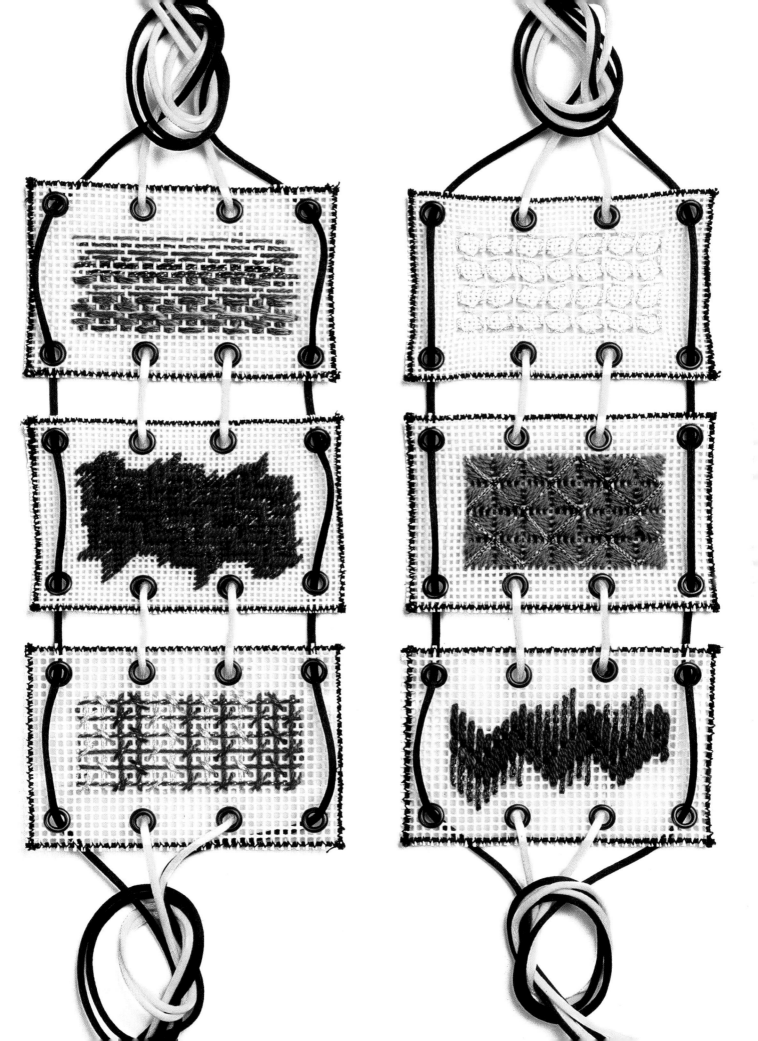

BORDERS

Borders present a different challenge and should enhance and, as a rule, bear some relationship to the design. Generally we think of a border as enclosing and completing a design, especially if it is a traditional geometric pattern or if there is a central device.

In some instances, a full surrounding border is too overpowering and does not allow the design to 'breathe', in which case a pair of simple side bands arranged either horizontally or vertically as though the whole design was part of an ongoing pattern may have more impact. A pair of bands either side of an embroidery also obviates the necessity for complex planning of the corners.

Egypt (Mary Pinch) emphasizes the face of Tutankhamun with a rice stitch, along with tent, satin, reversed tent, and a fishbone stitch border.

Corners

India (Gillian Bray) illustrates a
selection of border ideas (which
work separately or together)
incorporating herringbone, Jessica
stitches holding shisha mirrors,
twisted lattice band, long-armed
cross, tent, wheat sheaf circles, and
satin stitches and smyrna cross.

Once you have designed or decided on the border pattern, one of the most important features
is the corner design, which should match (unless you have deliberately planned otherwise). It is
not professional to 'fudge' a corner to make it match the others to cover up a mistake –
unfortunately, it will always stand out to haunt you once the work is completed. The proportions
of the border and the distance from the centre is a matter of personal choice and affected by
the size of the design or device; experimenting on sample pieces with pattern and colour to
achieve the right balance is a useful way of ensuring that you get it right.

If the border pattern is abstract or will not 'turn the corner' comfortably, it is possible to
manoeuvre out of this complication by squaring off the sides to form a corner square. This will
make a corner feature in which to use different stitches or devise a separate pattern to the size
of the square. The border or abstract pattern can be worked up the edge of the corner square
and, as long as it matches all round, it will not look contrived.

If the border design is an all-over pattern it will be possible to work horizontally across the work to the corner and then proceed down vertically without any problems. I suggest starting in the middle of one side of the design with the middle of a stitch or a repeat, checking as you go along each side that the pattern is correct and matches up with the opposite side.

Squares

It is helpful in the first instance to count and check that the number of threads on either side of the design are equal. If you have designed or decided on a pattern with repeats, you will be able to work out how many repeats will get you to the corner, or you can chart the design accordingly to turn at an appropriate point.

Bargello or any straight stitch patterns will generally turn and mitre neatly at the corner:

1. Start in the centre of one side at the lowest or highest point of the pattern and work to the corner diagonal mitre. Finish at this point.
2. Go to the adjacent side and, starting in the middle again, work to the mitre of the corner already half completed. The turn on the corner will form itself against the mitre.

If you prefer to plan exactly what pattern appears at the mitre, it will be necessary to plan and chart the stitches to relate to the number of threads in your border. A mirror placed at an angle over the stitches at any point will show you the resulting corner effect.

TIPS

- Straight stitches mitre on the diagonal.
- Diagonal stitches mitre on the straight.

Rectangles

Bargello or straight stitch for a rectangle will only mitre exactly on the corner if the longest side has been counted to incorporate a full repeat. If you are not prepared to count your longest side you can still make the corners match.

1. Start in the middle of your shortest side as described above and work to the mitre.
2. Turn 'on the mitre' and work down the long side.
3. Continue to work down the longest side but stop as the centre is approached.
4. On the opposite shortest side, repeat the process again, turning on the mitre and working nearly to the middle of the longest side again.

It will be possible to check the number of threads left to the centre point to see if the pattern is correct. If not, decide on a number of threads either side of the centre point and create a feature in the middle, either with a completely different pattern or a variety of stitches to fill the space. Because it will be the same on both long sides, it will look as if it is deliberate and, most importantly, all four corners will match.

BACKGROUND EFFECTS

You may stitch the background as you work the whole project or you may stitch it after the main design is completed. As with all best laid plans, once you have completed your main design it could be that the background requires a different treatment from the one you had planned. Don't be afraid to change your plan, as the textures and colours of your stitching might have brought a different depth and dimension to the whole project, requiring second thoughts for its background.

Whether your background recedes or dominates, it will rely not only on the stitch and thread but also the colour. A lighter background will throw up a central motif where a darker background will make it recede.

Canvas stitches

The most familiar solid background will be tent stitch. Being the smallest canvas work stitch, if you use thicker wools you will be able to fill in, shade or grade colours of any canvas background, making it eminently suitable for practical purposes. However tent stitch can also be worked in a variety of ways and with different threads so that an all-over open or delicate effect is achieved.

There are many other larger solid stitches that translate well for a uniform filled-in effect, such as cushion (Scotch) stitch and its prodigious range of variations. These can also be shaded to create a different effect. The design may lend itself to having a texture or pattern in the background with stitches such as double straight cross, rice stitch or crossed diamonds – the density of stitch will depend on the thread being used and whether you want the texture or pattern to be very obvious or not.

Spray-painted canvas textured with a decorative machine stitch pattern, overstitched with straight gobelin. The hand-made 'beads' are
a) machine-wrapped wire, hand rippled and coiled b) wound round a paper bead c) wound round a paper bead and waxed for additional texture.

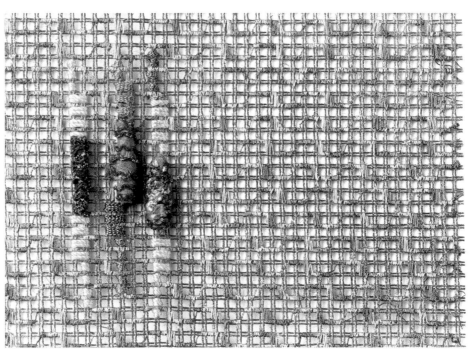

Diagonal stitches such as Byzantine, Oriental, Milanese, etc., worked across a background, can make the eye run off the design but, if you are depicting something that requires a diagonal stitch, change and vary the texture of thread so that the pattern is not all the same density.

An alternative is to divide the embroidery up into squares and work it four-dimensionally so that the diagonal stitches mitre on the vertical line. This can leave you with the feeling that the design is being absorbed by the background, so care should be taken with colours and the choice of thread to make sure that the design stands out.

Creating and imaging a specific effect such as water will easily be achieved with upright stitches, made all the more effective if the threads are varied so that there are different qualities in the stitch as it is formed. Breaking down the pattern randomly onto different levels will also make it more interesting and less rigid.

Textural backgrounds mixing a range of stitches will allow you to give reign to all sorts of creativity. It is important that it does not end up looking a mess, so plan to use stitches that will grow seamlessly in and out of each other, interspersed with areas of texture. For instance, a cushion (Scotch) stitch will easily transfer and move into a diagonal stitch, which starts with half a cushion stitch such as Milanese, Oriental or mosaic, etc. Smooth square stitches like the cushion will juxtapose with textured stitches such as Smyrna, Rhodes, etc.

Above
Box (Joan Hardingham) created using traditional canvas work stitches combined with beading and embroidery techniques worked in silks, ribbons, perles and machine embroidery threads.

Right
Sample (Jill Gibbs) showing satin stitches, long-armed cross, pattern darning, and reversed tent stitch worked to reveal the background of painted fusible webbing bonded onto the canvas.

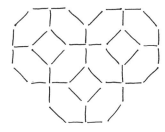

If stitched with a fine thread, a delicate effect will be achieved.

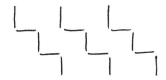

This pattern could be worked in any direction or stitched closer for a more dense effect.

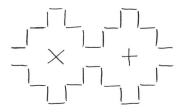

This all-over pattern will give a lightly textured open effect.

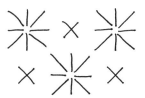

This simple pattern will give a textural, dense effect.

Pulled-thread stitches

Pulled-thread techniques will give you light and airy textures and background impressions, which could be used to complement a delicate design. Beads could be added for further embellishment. Patterns worked on the diagonal in trellis formations are very effective for surface texture (see photograph on page 81).

Diaper 'blackwork' patterns

Diaper patterns depending on the colour and thickness of the thread used would make an interesting open-textured and patterned background. It could be worked as a deliberate all-over pattern or disappear with thread the same colour as the background so that it looks like a self-patterned ground. Parts of the pattern could be left out or thickened accordingly (as you might in contemporary blackwork techniques) to give a less uniform overall impression.

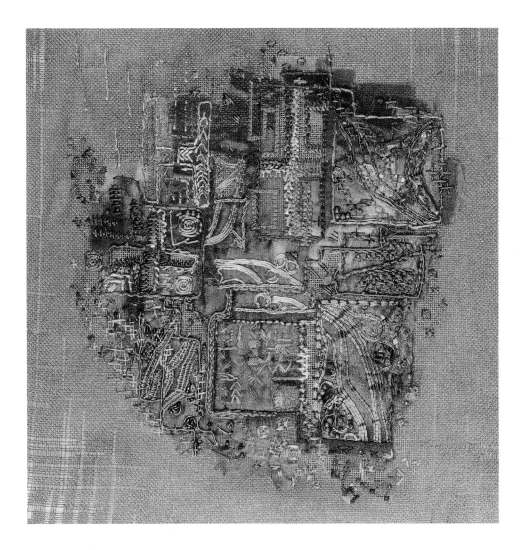

Random effects with only parts of the pattern or stitch worked will create abstract and open impressions. The strength of the emphasis is dependent on the thread being used – whether you want to 'make a statement' and deliberately plan to glimpse an interestingly painted or textured background.

Metal thread effects

Gold threads could be incorporated with laid fillings as a background effect and will introduce yet another dimension. Gold threads will generally stand out, so need to be used circumspectly. Depending on the design itself, it would be advisable to keep the laid filling fairly simple, otherwise the gold might dominate and swamp the main piece.

Beads

Beads can be added, if appropriate, to some background patterns, such as diaper patterns or pulled-thread stitches but you would need to consider the size carefully and also whether or not the beads would add or detract from the design.

Tiles (Mary Ann Morrison). Applied sheers, metal thread and couching techniques, beading, canvas and embroidery stitches have been combined to create the surface design of this textile.

With a thicker thread this pattern will become dense.

The spaces between the darning thread will create a more open effect with this pattern.

This will form a more definite pattern.

Darning for a pattern on the diagonal.

China (Mary Pinch) shows a diaper pattern and darning background. Other stitches include raised chain band, mosaic, and satin, with a fishbone stitch border.

Pattern darning

Pattern darning consists of running stitches being worked over and under a selected number of threads on the canvas. The patterns are usually formed with the straight darning stitches worked horizontally, vertically or diagonally. Pattern darning in its many forms – from the very simple 'staggering' or 'bricking' of broken lines of a specific length to the more complex structured decorative patterns – will offer you a simple but beautiful (and easy to do) textured background to offset rather than dominate a central design. The choice and colour of thread will change the effects dramatically and could be shaded in order to enhance the pattern itself and create interesting colour variations. Open darning patterns stitched with a thin thread as a background covering present a delicate textured effect. A close-packed darning pattern with a thicker thread will act as an interesting texture. On a painted background the thread has either to work as a contrast or to meld into the background.

Specific patterns, such as flower shapes, hearts, zigzags, etc., can be created and formed to cover an entire piece of work if appropriate. As these patterns are generally uniform and repetitive, it would make them more interesting to vary the texture by using different thicknesses of thread or to change the dimension of the pattern.

Alternatively, the darning stitches may be unmethodical with disparate lengths of stitch, and, instead of working them in an orderly fashion, you could work them randomly either on the straight or diagonally.

12 Finishing techniques

BLOCKING THE CANVAS

When you have finished your canvas work you will need to block and stretch it. This is important for straightening out any slight distortion of the canvas and for 'setting' the stitches to make the work look more even and professional. Stretching machines are now available specially for home use and, if you do a lot of canvas work, this may be a useful addition to your work room, or you may prefer to use professional blocking services. However, if you wish to stretch your own work, the following may be helpful.

1. Find a thick board larger than your canvas, soft enough to take drawing pins (thumb tacks) or rust-proof tacks.
2. Cover the board with old sheeting, stretched tightly and secured with tacks or staples. (Damping it and leaving it to dry on the board sometimes makes it more taut.)
3. Draw a grid of guidelines at 1 inch (25 mm) intervals using a secure waterproof pen.
4. Dampen the back of the completed canvas using a hand spray that sprays with a soft mist (not a jet). Be very careful if you have leather, other unusual items, gold thread or beads on the surface – in these circumstances, a good steam iron held above the back of the work may be sufficient dampening.
5. With the work right-side up, stretch and pin half of one side into position, lining it up straight against the grid. Repeat the process diagonally opposite on the other side. Work systematically round the work in this manner, going from one side to the other in order to keep the canvas square. Secure with the pins or tacks placed close together about ½ inch (13 mm) away from the finished design. You may have to readjust the canvas and reposition the drawing pins (thumb tacks) as you work, so do not push them in completely until you are sure the canvas is square against your grid.
6. Leave the board flat and allow to dry naturally, away from direct heat. When the project is completely dry, remove from the board.

FINISHING

How to finish off your canvas work is an important part of your planning and should be considered right at the beginning. The decision is easy for you when your project is going to be upholstered or used for soft furnishings as you will only need to leave seam allowances round your work. However, unless you are creating something practical, canvas work does not always have to be finished off so that the edges/selvedges are hidden, and there is no reason why you should not have some fun with the edges or make them a feature to create a unique finished piece.

Edges can be treated in a variety of ways but it is important to employ the technique appropriate to the type of canvas you are using.

Edging techniques. From left to right: Beaded open-sided square stitch/four-sided stitch/folded canvas tassel with a heading of machined close satin stitch; Decorative patterns machined on the folded edge/braid stitch/canvas tassel using tailor's tack foot for textured heading; Hem-stitched fringe/Fringe stitch/tassel with free machined cable stitch heading; Straight Gobelin in zig zag/buttonhole/folded canvas tassel with buttonhole heading.

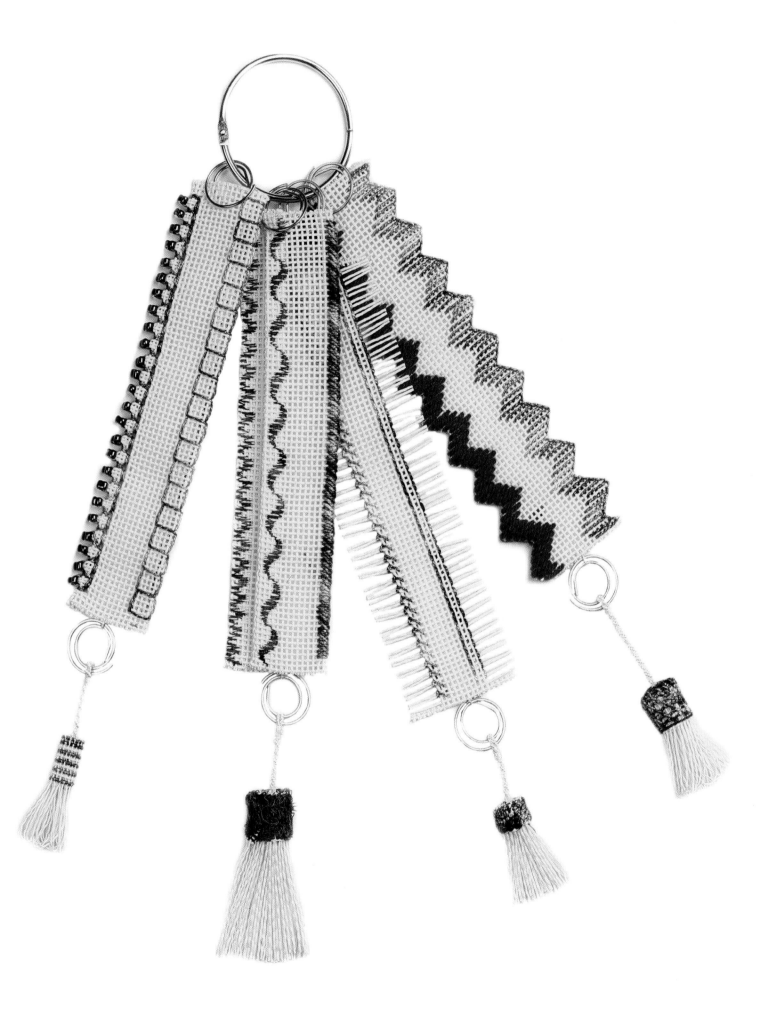

Bound edging

Canvas edges could be finished with a strong decorative binding stitch (not dissimilar to long-armed cross stitch), which gives the effect of a braid. It is easy to learn and adapts to most projects where an embellished edge is required. The thickness and type of thread used depends on the size of the canvas and effect required. The stitch can be worked on edges that have been folded over or left flat, and can also be used to join two seams.

CREATIVE IDEA

• Work two rows side by side to form a double decorative border.

Stitched

Four-sided stitch, hem stitch, picots with open-sided stitch and pin stitch are all pulled-thread techniques used on edges, which could be used to secure the edges of the canvas if a decorative hem is required.

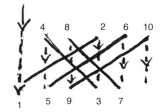

Binding stitch

Frayed

Fraying the edges of a finished piece is a simple and effective way of fringing and framing a piece of contemporary canvas work. This method will serve for panels as it obviates the need for hems or other decorative techniques, but would be impractical for most items.

On a project that is not static the threads could go on being snagged or pulled out of line unless they are trapped in place with stitching such as hem stitching, four-sided stitch (pulled-thread techniques) or fringe stitch. The line of stitching is made to the depth of the required length of fringe and before the edge is frayed out. The horizontal threads are then pulled away up to the stitched line, which will ensure that no more threads unravel and will also give you a decorative edge. Whether this edging is unobtrusive or a feature is a matter of choice and depends on the thread chosen for the stitching.

Apart from plastic or vinyl canvas, it is possible to fray out the edges of all the different types of canvas, but the effect varies because of the way the canvas is constructed. When the warp and weft threads are pulled away on a mono or double canvas, the effect in both directions is virtually the same. With the construction of an interlocking canvas, the effect of unravelling the edges is different on the warp side from the weft side. Try a test piece on your own canvas to check whether or not you like the effect.

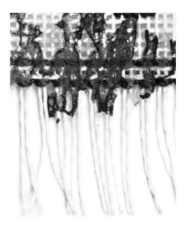

TIP

• If the canvas has been painted prior to the unravelling process, the fringe will probably require touching up, as very small unpainted specks may appear.

Fringed

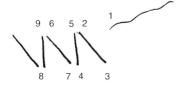

Fringe stich: Work from the wrong side of the fabric

Front side of fabric

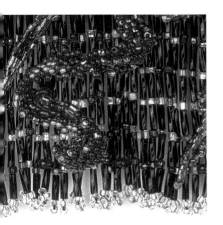

It is preferable to add threads to the edge of the work to form a proper decorative fringed edging. Unravelling enough of the canvas to knot or form into a fringe could be rather wasteful and the bunches will be rigid unless washed or dampened to get rid of the sizing, which is not always successful.

If you do not want to purchase a commercial fringe, simple fringes made of loops of thread may be added to the bottom of the work. These loops may be left as loops or cut, or a set number of the strands may be gathered up and knotted. The clusters of strands can be further developed by knotting, or they can be divided into larger clusters and wrapped at the neck to form tassels. The most basic and effective method is simply to add loops of double thickness thread to the bottom of the work. Use a crochet hook to pull the loop of double thread through the canvas, and hook the loose ends through the loop.

BEADED FRINGES

Fringes made of beads will swing and bring sparkle and pizzazz to your project. The fringe can be as long or as short as necessary, random lengths, made up of a multiple selection of beads, or all the same type. Secure the sewing thread in the canvas before threading a selection of beads onto the needle. Return back up through the entire length of beads and attach the line to the edge of the canvas before the subsequent line of beads is threaded. The choice of beads is electrifying and generally irresistible – square, round, hexagonal, shiny, matt, facetted, and more.

Develop the concept further by picking up elements of your design for a beaded fringe:

1. To create the patterned bead fringe draw your design in colour onto a strip of paper, making it exactly the same size as the required length and width of the fringe.
2. Choose the appropriate size of beads for the finished fringe.
3. Use a piece of cotton tape, braid or suitable fabric for the heading. Secure the thread in the tape and, working with your stitching thread held over the top of your design, add beads onto the thread to match the design. Follow the shapes and the correct colour sequence.
4. At the end of each line, lay the beaded thread over the top of the design and push the beads up closely to check that you have them in the correct order.
5. At the end of the fringe, return back through the last bead and up the line for extra strength, and make an overstitch in the braid before collecting up the beads for the next line. Make the lines of beads sit as close as possible to each other so that the design is not lost.
6. The tape can then be incorporated and hidden in the bottom seam. Alternatively, follow the same method, but stitch straight into the finished seam edge of the item onto which you are attaching the fringe.

Machine stitching

When appropriate to the design, open or closed zigzag satin stitches will finish off the edges of canvas. If you have a machine with an exciting choice of decorative patterns, some of these may be appropriate for edging the canvas, but you will need to experiment on sample pieces to check the effect is what you want and that it will be successful as an edging to your design.

Embroidery stitches

- Threads could be **couched** on the edges for a decorative finish if the piece is not going to be used for a practical purpose.
- **Buttonhole stitch** edging could be worked invisibly in either straight or zigzag lines to contain the threads on the edges with straight canvas work stitches worked over the top.
- More prominence and a feature could be made of a buttonhole edge by wrapping it with a thicker thread to make it look like a cord, or it could be worked like a Hardanger edging technique where the threads are cut away from blocks of buttonhole stitching.

Canvas work stitches

Simple straight stitches either in undulating lines or sharp points can be worked on the edge of a piece of canvas. Prepare and stabilize the edge first by machining it with straight or small open zigzag stitches. If you are still uncertain that this will hold, gently dab PVA or similar glue on the edge of the canvas threads after the machining and before the hand stitching.

Fabric

If it is considered an integral part of the design, bands of fabric could be incorporated with the project either to add on the edges or to enclose it. This is particularly useful if you wish to inset a piece for something like a cushion. The inset width has to be determined in proportion to the size of canvas work, and this is very often a matter of personal choice and governed by the finished size required. Usually piping is used on the edge of a cushion and this can be echoed inside the inset to highlight the embroidery. Generally the fabric should be backed to bring it to the equivalent weight of the canvas embroidery so that it 'sits' properly.

Making up bags by adding bands of fabric to your canvas work is particularly satisfying as it presents the opportunity to choose colours to enhance or contrast with your design. Bands may be added all round or just top and/or bottom. Making up a bag in this way means that you do not have bulky canvas seams to contend with.

PRESENTATION

Opposite
Spot motif with close zigzag holding the fringe and cut threads; twisted threads (Hardanger technique) hold the unusual button in position.

How your work is presented depends on the project in hand. Having spent many hours and care on your project, do not spoil it by stinting on your presentation.

TIP

- Always take the time to work one or two lines of tent stitching round your finished piece so that no canvas shows, should the framing or stitching not be exact.

Panels

If your work is to be a panel, do not just rely on the professional framer to know what you want. Your design needs to 'breathe', so do not cramp it with a bold or heavy frame unless that is the effect you are looking for. Decide whether or not the panel is to have a mount, whether the mount is to be plain or fabric-covered card and how big it should be in relation to the piece of work. If your canvas is very raised or highly textured, it may require a box effect with a deep frame and spacers under the frame to keep the glass away from it, should you be using glass. Although unglazed work is the ideal, depending on your circumstances and the project in hand, it may be necessary to glaze. Try to choose a frame that enhances your work, does not dominate it and has some relation to the colours of the embroidery.

If the panel does not lend itself to being enclosed with a surface surround, it could be mounted 'proud' onto a larger card, board or fabric-covered background. You would need to lace the canvas to suitable card or board and then attach it to the background. Check what you can see down the side edges if you choose a thick card over which to lace. Ensure that the design follows continuously from the front over the sides and does not end untidily in a random way on the edge. When you frame in this manner, it may be more effective not to have a commercial frame round the whole work, but simply to leave it free.

Cushions

There are many different and innovative ways of making up cushions and it is worth visiting relevant stores, looking at up-to-date magazines and books on soft furnishings to give you some new and contemporary ideas for finishing and presenting your cushion. If your design is small, it may be more effective to inset it with a fabric border so that it is the central focus and not wasted curving off down the sides.

Left
Bag (Jill Carter) developing the bar code theme into a project with double-tied oblong cross, pattern darning, reversed cushion and long-armed cross stitches. Machined threads form a braid handle and the turk's head fastening is made from machined wrapped thread.

TIP

- Choose a cushion pad 1 inch (2.5 cm) larger than the finished design for a rounded shape.

Boxes

To make hand-made boxes is a specialized skill and stitching a canvas to incorporate into boxes needs careful forward planning. The design needs to be thoroughly thought out for the shape of box you are making. Measurements need to be exact and the choice of canvas is very important. A badly joined seam of bulky canvas will definitely spoil the look of your box. Insetting canvas into fabric ensures the seams will be easier to join neatly. Alternatively, a piece of canvas may be inset in a specially purchased wooden box or coaster, etc., where all the pieces will have been made, and you simply insert your finished piece.

Upholstery

Generally any of the difficult decisions over canvas and thread are made for you and determined by the size and choice of furniture for which you are stitching. Always leave a good 2-3 inches (5-7.5 cm) round any piece of work that is going to be upholstered so that there is something to pull on, and work only on the very best canvas for longevity. Consider carefully what threads you use if you want your piece to last. Ensure that you are confident you have found a competent upholsterer who understands the vagaries of textiles, and never give your masterpiece to an upholsterer whom you have not tried or tested on previous items.

Cords

Where appropriate, purchased or hand-made cords will enhance or finish off seams or edges, but try not to use them to cover up bad seam stitching. Making your own cords is not difficult and gives you the option of including some of the threads already used in the work. It is now possible to buy cord winders for using in the home. They are tremendous fun and more than pay for themselves, as you will suddenly want to make cords for everything. The winder will come with instructions for basic cord making, but there are also some wonderfully inspiring books to encourage you to be more adventurous with cords.

Folded canvas tassel with a buttonhole heading and machine-wrapped cord.

Tassels

Tassels of any type are a great decorative addition to canvas work for texture or to 'make a statement'. If you do not have extensive skills in tassel-making techniques, a simple tassel formed round card will fit the bill. Consider your threads carefully, either to match or contrast with your embroidery. Some gold threads will be stiff and may make the tassel look rigid. Mixing cotton threads with some shiny textures will prevent the cotton strands sticking to each other and give the tassel a more fluid movement. Machine embroidery threads are excellent for fine or small tassels.

Tassels can also be made from the canvas:

1. Decide on the dimension of the tassel – whether it should be fat or thin, long or short - and cut a rectangle of canvas according to your measurements.
2. Leave 6 – 8 threads (according to the depth of the tassel 'heading' required) at the top and bottom of the rectangle.
3. Pull out horizontal threads of canvas in between and up to the heading.
4. Fold in half and securely stitch the chosen cord through both thicknesses and close to the edge of the heading.
5. Lightly glue with PVA the top six to eight threads and roll up the rectangle.
6. Leave to stick and dry before stitching the buttonhole heading.
7. Using a single thread, start by wrapping it a couple of times anti-clockwise round the base of the heading and work a row of buttonhole stitches onto this wrap. This is the foundation of your decorative heading so the stitches need to be neat and evenly spaced.
8. Work subsequent rows of buttonhole stitch into each previous row (as for needle lace techniques) and work up the heading until you have reached the top.
9. To shape the top, decrease the stitches by working into alternate buttonhole loops until you have reached the centre. Finish off with some backstitches and take the thread down through the centre of the heading to be lost in the tassel.

Fabric

Prairie points taken from patchwork techniques add another dimension to finishing off canvas work as a fabric edging – perhaps on the bottom of a bag or to edge an inset. They can be worked to any size, and rows may be added to rows.

Stitches

Back: single & double threaded

Bullion knot or stitch

Twisted chain

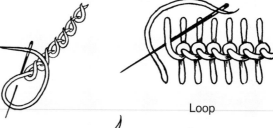

Loop

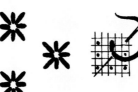

Portuguese knotted stem

Double knot

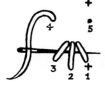

Back

Buttonhole or blanket

Algerian eye

Palestrina

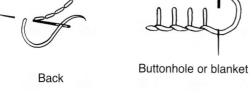

Open chain

Knotted chain

Bokhara couching

Open cretan

Fly

Whipped chain

Roumanian couching

Split

Spider web

Crown

Lock

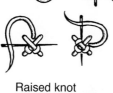

Portuguese knotted stem

Raised knot

Thorn

French knot

Hardanger stitch diagrams by Siriol Clarry, taken from *Hardanger Embroidery* by Jill Carter (Batsford, 2000). Shisha stitch diagrams taken from *The Batsford Encyclopaedia of Embroidery Stitches* by Anne Butler (Batsford, 1979). Half Rhodes and Norwich/Waffle taken from *Dictionary of Canvas Work Stitches* by Mary Rhodes (Batsford, 1980). All other stitch diagrams taken from *Embroidery Stitches* by Barbara Snook (Batsford, 1963). See opposite page for Jessica stitch.

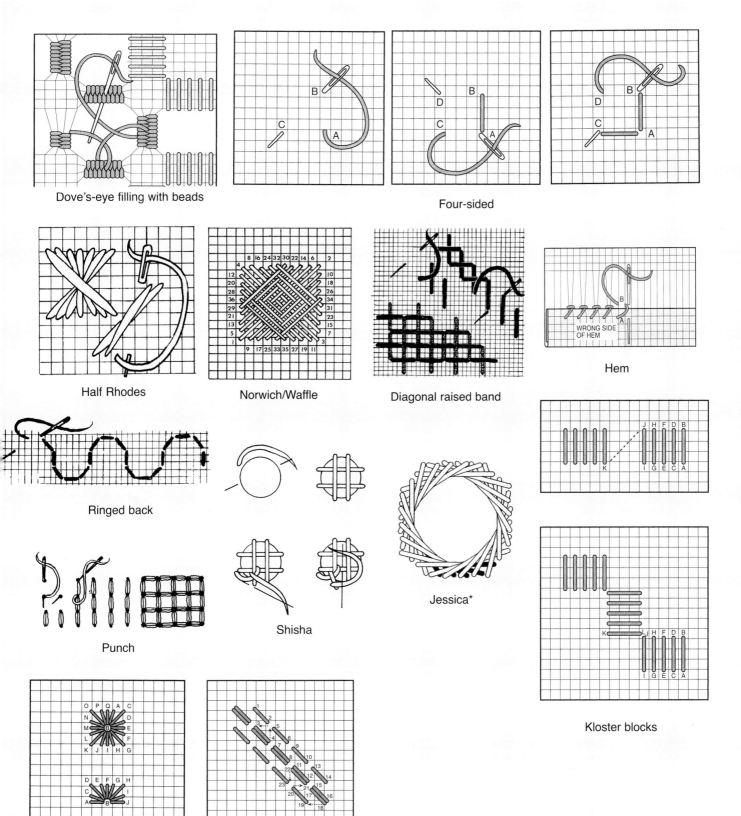

Dove's-eye filling with beads

Four-sided

Half Rhodes

Norwich/Waffle

Diagonal raised band

Hem

WRONG SIDE OF HEM

Ringed back

Shisha

Jessica*

Punch

Kloster blocks

Square eyelet

Reversed diagonal faggoting

* Publisher's note: The Jessica stitch was first published in *Needlepoint Stitches* by Jean Hilton (1988). Jean Hilton is a canvas work designer in the USA. Jessica stitch diagram above taken from *The Needlepoint Book* by Jo Ippolito Christensen (Simon & Schuster, 1999).

EQUIPMENT AND MATERIALS

United Kingdom

Art Van Go
The Studios
1 Stevenage Road
Knebworth
Hertfordshire SG3 6AN
email: art@artvango.co.uk
(Angelina, wireform, metal shim)

The Bead Merchant
PO Box 5025
Coggeshall,
Essex C06 1HW
Tel: 08706 093 036
(Wide range and selection of all types of beads)

Designer Yarns Ltd
Units 8-10 Newbridge Industrial Estate
Pitt Street
Keighley
West Yorkshire BD21 4PQ
Tel: 01353 664222
(Textured and novelty knitting yarns)

DMC Creative World Ltd
Pullman Road
Wigston
Leicestershire LE18 2DY
Tel: 0116 281 1040
www.dmc.com
(For stockists of threads and canvas)

London Bead Company
339 Kentish Town Road
London NW5 2 TJ
Tel: 0870 203 2323/0207 284 2062
(Beads, canvas. wide variety of embroidery threads)

Mulberry Silks
Silkwood
4 Park Close
Tedbury
Gloucestershire GL8 8HS
Tel: 01666 503 438
www.mulberrysilks-patriciawood.com
email: patricia.wood@rdplus.net
(Silk threads for hand and machine embroidery)

Sue Hawkins
Needlworks
East Wing
Highfield House
Whitminster GL2 7PJ
Tel: 01452 740118
email: sue@suehawkins.com
(Specialist upholstered embroidery frames)

Oliver Twists Threads Ltd
22 Phoenix Road
Crowther Industrial Estate
Washington
Tyne and Wear NE38 OAD
Tel: 0191 416 6016
email: jean@olivertwists.freeserve.co.uk
(Hand dyed threads, fabrics and fibres)

Sew-It-All Ltd
The Warehouse.
24 Chandos Road
Buckingham MK18 1AL
Tel: 0800 7314563 or
0044 (0) 1280 821 777
E-mail: info@sewitall.co.uk
(Canvas and even weave fabrics)

The Silk Route
Cross Cottage
Cross Lane,
Frimley Green
Surrey GU16 6LN
Tel: 01252 835 781
www.thesilkroute.co.uk
(Fabric - Silks, tissues, organzas and texture packs)

West End Embroidery
Orchid Cottage
Drury Lane
Mortimer Common
Reading
Berkshire RG7 2JN
Tel: 01189 332 670
www.WestEndEmbroidery.com
(Lowery workstands, accessories, canvas, threads)

USA

Stitchers' Paradise
The Cross Stitch Station
18 SW 8th Street
Miami, FL 33130 USA
Tel: (305) 372 3717
www.stitchers-paradise.com
(Suppliers of everything related to canvas work embroidery)

Needle Nook of La Jolla
7719 Fay Avenue
La Jolla, CA 92037 USA
Tel: (858) 459-1711
1-800-685-1711
email: ndlpoint@needlenookoflajolla.com
Fax: (858) 459-9536

The Edwardian Needle
225 Belleville Avenue
Bloomfield, New Jersey 07003 USA
Tel: (973) 743-9833
Fax: (973) 680-1162
email: info@theedwardianneedle.com
www.theedwardianneedle.com

Australia and New Zealand

The Crewel Gobelin
9 Marian Street
Killara
NSW 2071
Australia
Tel: 00 61 (0) 2 94986831

Total Image Embroidery
485 Sloane Street
Te Awamutu
New Zealand
Tel: 07 870 4258

Nancy's Embroidery Shop
273 Tinakori Road
(PO Box 245)
Wellington
New Zealand
Tel: 04 473 4047
Fax: 04 473 0919
Email: nancys@actrix.gen.nz

Woolly Valley & The Embroidery Shop
4-12 Cruckshank St
Kilbirnie
PO Box 14-266
Kilbirnie
Wellington
New Zealand
Tel: 04 387 8996
Fax: 04 387 8345
Email: mcetten@xtra.co.nz
www.kraftykiwis.co.nz

Yarns – Kathy McLauchlan
2 Puketai Place
Pukerua Bay
Porirua
New Zealand
Tel: 04 239 9851
Email: mclpad@xtra.co.nz

NB: All NZ phone numbers are internal NZ only.
Outside NZ, add 00 64, and drop the first 0.

FURTHER READING

The Needlepoint Book Jo Ippolito Christensen (revised edition) (Fireside Simon &
Schuster, 1999)

Father B's 21st Century Book of Stitches The Rev. Robert E Blackburn, Jr (6th edition) (
Rainbow Gallery, 2000)

The Ultimate Encyclopedia of Canvas Embroidery Jane D Zimmerman (All volumes self-
published)

The Open Canvas Carolyn Ambuter (Workman Publishing Co., 1982)

Beginners' Guide to Machine Embroidery Pam Watts (Search Press, 2003)

Machine Embroidery Stitch Techniques Valerie Campbell-Harding and Pamela Watts
(Batsford, 1989)

Index

A
Automatic patterns 88
Angelina 28
Attaching objects 67

B
Bar codes 34, 40
Background effects 111
Background stitching 106
Beads 92, 96, 98,102,114
Beads with Hardanger 105
Beads with pulled thread 104
Beaded fringes 119
Binding stitch 118
Blocking 116
Borders 108, 110
Bound edgings 118
Box stitches 103
Boxes 122
Buttonhole 63, 69, 98, 124

C
Canvas 8,76
Cable stitch 84, 90
Colour 30, 32, 74
Colour and stitch 33, 74
Composite stitches 58
Computer-aided design 38
Cords 122
Corners 109
Couching 48, 49
Cross stitch 102
Cushions 121

D
Design 34
Diaper patterns 113
Diagonal stitches 102, 112
Drawn thread 71, 92
Drinking straws 64

E
Eyelets 94
Edgings 118, 119, 120
Embroidery stitches 52, 120

F
Fabric 22, 120, 122
Fabric paints 20
Finishing 116
Frames 14
Frayed edging 118

Free machining 88, 89
Fringed edgings 119
Fusible webbing 25

G
Granite stitch 53, 90

H
Hardanger 73

I
Individual stitches 56
Irregular shapes 67

K
Knots 56
Knotted line stitches 54

L
Laid fillings 48
Laid grid 67
Laying tools 16
Leather 60
Line stitches 52

M
Machine edgings 120
Machine stitching 26
Machining on net 94
Metal thread effects 114
Mirrors 62

N
Needles 14
Needleweaving 69, 71

P
Painted backgrounds 18
Panels 121
Paper 10, 23
Paper tubes 64
Pattern darning 115
Presentation 121
Progressing your skills 36
Pulled thread 76, 78, 81, 113

R
Raffia 10
Rectangles 110
Repeating patterns 38
Ribbon 23

S
Screenprinting 21
Shisha stitch 68, 125
Silk fabrics 23
Silk 'paper' 24
Sinamai 28
Sizoflor 28
Squares 110
Stands 16
Stitches 40-45, 124, 125
Sticks 67
Straight stitches 102
Straight stitch machining 83, 89

T
Tassels 123
Tent stitch 98, 101, 111
Textures 22, 26
Transfer paints 19
Transferring designs 17
Threads 12, 73, 77
Three dimensional effects 94
Tied stitches 102

U
Using the machine 82
Upholstery 122

W
Water-soluble effects 94
Wire 10, 29
Wire 'beads' 64

Z
zigzag machining 85, 87, 91-2